WORLD BANK STAFF OCCASIONAL PAPERS □ NUMBER TWENTY-SIX

Susan Hill Cochrane

Fertility and Education

What Do We Really Know?

Published for the World Bank
The Johns Hopkins University Press
Baltimore and London

Library of Congress Cataloging in Publication Data

Cochrane, Susan Hill, 1943–
  Fertility and education.
  (World Bank staff occasional papers ; 26)
  Bibliography: p. 153
  Includes index.
  1. Fertility, Human. 2. Education.
3. Family size. I. Title. II. Series.
HB903.F4C58   301.32'1   78-26070
ISBN 0-8018-2140-1 pbk.

Foreword

•-•--•-•-•

I would like to explain why the World Bank does research work and why this research is published. We feel an obligation to look beyond the projects that we help finance toward the whole resource allocation of an economy and the effectiveness of the use of those resources. Our major concern, in dealings with member countries, is that all scarce resources—including capital, skilled labor, enterprise, and know-how—should be used to their best advantage. We want to see policies that encourage appropriate increases in the supply of savings, whether domestic or international. Finally, we are required by our Articles, as well as by inclination, to use objective economic criteria in all our judgments.

These are our preoccupations, and these, one way or another, are the subjects of most of our research work. Clearly, they are also the proper concern of anyone who is interested in promoting development, and so we seek to make our research papers widely available. In doing so, we have to take the risk of being misunderstood. Although these studies are published by the Bank, the views expressed and the methods explored should not necessarily be considered to represent the Bank's views or policies. Rather, they are offered as a modest contribution to the great discussion on how to advance the economic development of the underdeveloped world.

ROBERT S. McNAMARA
President
The World Bank

Contents

•⊙•

TABLES

FIGURES

Preface

•●•

Throughout the past decade interest has been growing both in understanding the socioeconomic forces that cause fertility to fall during the process of economic development and in devising policies that might harness these forces to accelerate the decline. Among the factors most commonly emphasized as important—and one which is tractable to policy manipulation—is education.

In many situations there is an apparently inverse relation between the level of educational attainment and fertility. Closer examination shows, however, that this inverse relation is not invariant. Without a detailed understanding of the numerous channels through which education may act, it is impossible to understand why education and fertility are usually, but not always, inversely related. Previous reviews of the effect of education on fertility have not explored how education affects fertility.

Thus, although the first chapter of this book contains a review of the evidence on the relation, the principal contribution of the study lies in its attempt to link education to the more direct determinants of fertility such as age of marriage, desired family size, and contraceptive knowledge. A model of how education acts through these intervening variables is presented, after which the empirical evidence on the relations between education and the determinants of fertility is reviewed. The final chapter summarizes the evidence supporting the model and provides a guide for identifying those areas in which additional research is needed.

This project was begun while I was at the World Bank for a year as a Brookings economic policy fellow and has been completed since I joined the staff of the Bank. I appreciate the opportunity that these institutions offered me to undertake such a rewarding project. I should like to thank Timothy King especially for suggesting the project to me and for encouraging its publication. He and other members of the Division of Population and Human Resources provided helpful suggestions at many stages. I should also like to thank Dov Chernichovsky, Ali Khan, and Donald J. O'Hara for their detailed comments. In addition, two anonymous reviewers of the manuscript provided exceptionally constructive suggestions for revision.

Kalpana Nandwani and Miren Etcheverry provided invaluable help with editing and proofing, and Sue Thavamoney gave continuous assistance in typing the many drafts. I am grateful for these efforts.

Virginia deHaven Orr edited the final manuscript, Brian J. Svikhart supervised the design and production of the book, and Christine Houle prepared the author index.

SUSAN HILL COCHRANE

March 1979
Washington, D.C.

Fertility and Education

What Do We Really Know?

Introduction and Summary

The inverse relationship of education to completed family size is one of the most clearcut correlations found in the literature

MCGREEVEY AND BIRDSALL (1974)[1]

An increase in income causes an increase in education. And parental education in LDC's reduces fertility, this much is clear from both cross-national and intracountry cross-sections.

SIMON (1974)

With regard to education attainment, we hypothesized that: The higher the educational level of the husband and wife, the lower the fertility. There is certainly overwhelming empirical evidence for this hypothesis.

MASON AND OTHERS (1971)

Such a consensus on the relation between two variables is extremely rare in the social sciences. Does such a well-accepted relation provide the information necessary to design policies to reduce fertility?

1. References are indicated in the text by the author's name and date of publication in parenthesis. Complete reference citations for each chapter are given in the sources.

Several pragmatic economists have maintained that if a functional relation between two variables is very stable, then, assuming causation can be established, one variable can be manipulated to alter the other. More important, they maintain that these manipulations can be used whether or not the underlying theory and structure of factors causing the relation are understood. If this argument and the consensus on the education-fertility relation above are accepted, it could be argued that education should be increased to reduce fertility. This is, in fact, what is generally argued.

There are several problems with this approach. Even if the relation between education and fertility is assumed to be universally inverse and stable, something about what causes the two to interact in this manner still needs to be known. Specifically, to design educational policies in an effective and efficient manner, the elements of the educational process that lead to lower fertility[2] and the possibility of simulating these effects quickly and inexpensively through mass media campaigns or small group "consciousness sessions," such as in China, need to be known. Since there is no consensus on how education causes fertility reduction, however, these issues remain unresolved.

In addition to questions of how to replicate the effects of education on fertility inexpensively, some serious questions exist concerning the atypical cases in which there are no relations between the two variables, curvilinear effects, or even positive relations. Mason and others (1971) noted eight such atypical cases in a review of thirty-two studies; Simon (1974) and McGreevey and Birdsall (1974) cite additional ones. One researcher who has studied the Philippines has even concluded that "at the earlier stages of economic development . . . rising levels of income and education merely aggravate the population problem" (Encarnación, 1974). Therefore, the evidence on the relation between education and fertility must be reexamined to determine what causes the general inverse relation and what explains the deviant cases. Such a review will give a clearer picture of what kind of research is needed to design effective, efficient policies to reduce fertility.

---

2. The acquisition of literacy, job skills, new values, or new information could cause education to have its negative effects on fertility.

Structure of the Study

The first kind of evidence reviewed summarizes current research on the relation between education and fertility. That review determines the uniformity of the relation and develops a topology for the atypical cases. As stated above, however, it is not enough simply to know if a relation exists; the factors causing it must also be understood. The rest of the volume investigates how education acts through other variables to bring about reductions in fertility. This is particularly important, since education by itself cannot directly affect actual fertility behavior but must act through factors such as preferences for large families, knowledge of birth control, health of parents and children, and so forth.

A model relating these intervening variables to fertility is developed, and a set of hypotheses is generated regarding the relation between education and these intervening variables and through them to fertility. The evidence on these relations is then systematically reviewed.

Selection of Evidence

Before summarizing the results of this survey, the basis for selecting studies that are included in the review should be explained. First, both group and individual data are reviewed. If an individual's fertility was affected only by that individual's education, then data pertaining only to individuals and households would be necessary. There is some evidence, however, that the aggregate level of education in the community, as well as an individual's education, affects the level of fertility. Ideally, individual fertility should be studied using both individual and aggregate levels of education together to explain the relations. Although some work is currently being done on this, not much of it is published. Therefore, aggregate and individual data must be examined separately.

To decide which research should be included in the review, a choice had to be made between including only those studies of impeccable methodology and including a larger number of studies of varying methodological standards; the latter course was chosen. Although some research is excluded because it lacks minimally acceptable controls, studies using simple, nonrigorous methodology or small samples, as well as studies using highly sophisticated methodology and large samples, are included. Such a situation raises some problems in comparing the studies. It was felt, however, that these complications were outweighed by the need to study the relations in as many different countries as possible. Since the poorest countries have the most limited supply of data, restricting attention to studies with large samples and rigorous methodology would have limited the geographic coverage of this review. Even imposing very minimal restrictions limited the data on several topics. For example, no appropriate research could be found on Sub-Saharan Africa, so the relation between education and contraceptive use for women of different ages could not be examined. Therefore, in the various studies, the limitations of the data will be mentioned as the results are reported.

The Empirical Relation

Many studies relating national or regional levels of education and fertility showed significant inverse relations. Many other studies, however, showed no significant relation, mixed evidence of significantly inverse and significantly direct relations, or evidence only of a significant positive relation. In general, the evidence of an inverse relation between education and fertility in aggregate data is strongest for countries at the middle level of development.

Because of these mixed results, the aggregate data do not allow policy prescriptions to be developed. It is possible that the deviant cases in the aggregated relation result, not because education fails to reduce fertility at the individual level, but because this relation becomes blurred when individuals are grouped together by geographic area. This can be determined if the evidence on the relation between education and fertility at the individual level for developing countries is examined. Two of the most obvious generalizations resulting from studies of individuals are that the inverse relation is much more consistent for female than male education and for urban rather than rural areas. This might lead to the recommendation that educational efforts be concentrated on the women in the urban sector. Closer examination of the data, however, indicates that uniformly inverse relations between education and fertility are also more likely in countries with moderately high female literacy rates. In some countries with low levels of female literacy, fertility tends to be higher among women with a small amount of education than among women with no schooling. Before policy recommendations can be developed from this evidence, it is necessary to determine the mechanisms that cause both the positive and negative relations observed.

To develop policy recommendations, all economists would agree that at least the direction of causation must be established: does education cause fertility to be what it is, does fertility affect education, or does some other unidentified factor affect both education and fertility? Only in the first instance can educational policy be used successfully to alter fertility.

The fact that two variables tend to be closely associated and move together does not necessarily mean that one affects the behavior of the other. The existence of a causal relation and the direction of causation are not easily established even in laboratory situations. At a minimum, the way (or ways) in which one variable may affect the other must be established. The model developed in this book is designed to trace out the channels through which education may act. Evidence supporting many of these channels is given in the second half of the book, but the entire causal model cannot be said to be definitively proved by these results, and the importance of other factors that affect the relation between education and fertility explains why the relation is not always inverse.

Channels through which Education Affects Fertility

An economic model of fertility has been developed to determine how education affects fertility. In this model it is hypothesized that education does not affect fertility directly, but that it acts through many variables. The model hypothesizes that fertility is determined by the biological supply of children, by the demand for children by husbands and wives, and by the regulation of fertility. The most important supply effects of education are hypothesized to be those influencing the proportion married or probability of marriage, age of marriage, and health, particularly infant and child mortality. The most important demand effects appear to be the effect of education on the perceived costs and benefits of children and on family size preferences. While the effect of education on the wife's market wage and occupation is hypothesized to affect greatly the demand for children, there are not enough data available to establish conclusively the relation between such variables and fertility in developing countries. There are more data on the effect of the husband's income on fertility, but it is very ambiguous. Education is expected to have a substantial effect on fertility through its effect on fertility regulation. It is hypothesized that education is related to favorable attitudes toward birth control, improved knowledge of birth control, and better communication between husband and wife. Through these variables, education should lead to greater use of contraception, other things being equal.

Education and the Biological Supply of Children

Data show that education can both increase and decrease the potential biological supply of surviving children. The increases occur because education is associated with better health and consequently great fecundity: that is, higher probabilities of conceiving. Better education of parents is also associated with lower infant and child mortality, particularly in countries with intermediate levels of mortality. Education tends to decrease the potential biological supply of births because it is associated with older ages of first marriage and thus fewer years of exposure to pregnancy. This effect of education on age of marriage is stronger for women than for men. But the effect of education on the probability of ever marrying appears to vary from society to society.

Education and the Demand for Children

Education is hypothesized primarily to decrease the demand for children, and the evidence seems to support this inverse relation. Education also decreases the ideal family size, but there are a few exceptions. Education greatly decreases the perceived benefits of children in several surveys in Asia. It also appears to increase the sensitivity to the cost of children. But, in a cross-cultural study in Asia, education also was shown to increase the perceived ability to afford children. Since education reduces infant and child mortality and raises the supply of living children, it will reduce the demand for additional births unless it increases the desired family size as much as, or more than, it increases the supply of surviving children.

Education, through all these factors, generally decreases the demand for children as measured by desired family size, but there are a number of cases in which there is no relation or in which the relation is not uniform. There are not enough data to generalize about sex differences or urban-rural differences in the effect of education on demand factors. There is also insufficient evidence on the relation between fertility and education, wife's wages, and compatibility of market work in developing countries.

Education and Fertility Regulation

The ambiguities associated with the effect of education on fertility acting through the biological supply of children and, to a lesser extent, the demand for children do not exist with respect to fertility regulation. Education has positive effects on attitudes toward contraception, knowledge of contraception, and communication between husband and wife and, through these and other variables, on contraceptive usage. Thailand in 1969–70 is the only country that had unexplained deviations from the expected pattern, but by 1976 these deviations had largely disappeared. Thus, the most consistent effect of education seems to be on fertility regulation. This does not mean that other factors are unimportant for desired family size, and the desire for an additional child is important in explaining actual contraceptive use.

Summary

The evidence seems to indicate that education may increase or decrease individual fertility. The decrease is greater for the education of women than of men and in urban than rural areas. But education is more likely to increase fertility in countries with the lowest level of female literacy. Although the evidence is not conclusive, since there are not enough studies in the least literate societies, it appears that education initially increases the ability to have live births, probably through improved health, better nutrition, and the abandoning of traditional patterns of lactation and postpartum abstinence. Initially, this effect seems to be strong enough to counteract the effect of education on the postponement of marriage. In societies with higher average levels of female literacy, education lowers the demand for children by altering their perceived costs and benefits. In addition, once the biological supply of children exceeds the demand for them, high levels of education enable couples to limit their fertility more efficiently through more access to contraceptive knowledge and improved ability to communicate with each other.

Several questions need further research, however. The first question is the effect of aggregate literacy rates on individual behavior. The difference in the individual education and fertility relation observed at high and low levels of literacy may be caused by such effects. Alternatively, differences in literacy levels may simply reflect the level of development. A more probable explanation is that some of the aggregate effects of education depend on the level of development, and others in fact depend on aggregate levels of literacy. A second question that needs to be resolved is why the inverse relation between education and fertility tends to exist more in urban than in rural areas. A third puzzle, the reason for the differing effects of male and female education, has been discussed extensively in this study. The question remains imperfectly solved, however, in part because of the limited number of studies on the education of males and their fertility and on other related variables such as desired family size, contraceptive knowledge, and health. Many of these issues can be resolved by analyzing the data from the World Fertility Survey being conducted in over thirty-five developing countries under the auspices of the International Statistical Institute.

1

The Empirical Relation

     The relation between education and fertility has been examined since the beginning of the study of economics and of demography. Malthus and his successors in both fields have proposed numerous theories about why more education is usually associated with lower fertility. But these theories have not been complex enough to account for atypical cases. Whether the simple theories explain a situation sufficiently depends on the frequency of atypical cases and the use to be made of the relation. This chapter reviews a broad range of studies relating education to fertility, and the evidence shows that the relation is not as uniform as is generally believed. Many cases exist where education is either unrelated to fertility or is actually positively related. Thus, any attempt to use the relation between education and fertility for policy purposes requires a better understanding of the circumstances in which an inverse relation is likely to arise and why it does not arise in other circumstances. This chapter addresses only the first question. The mechanisms through which education affects fertility and the reasons why its effect may be positive or negative under various circumstances will be examined extensively in the next chapter.

Two kinds of evidence are reviewed here. First, studies that compare the average fertility and average education of geographical aggregates of people (countries, or subregions within countries) are presented. The second type of study examines the relation between individual education and fertility.

Aggregate Studies

The data needed to study the average levels of education and fertility among geographic groupings of people come from two sources, censuses and vital registration systems.

Data from censuses

Census data is collected periodically on the number of people in a country, their age, sex, location, and certain other characteristics such as education, occupation, and so forth. Education data in a census may include current enrollment, literacy, and years of school completed. Such information is often reported separately for males and females.

Fertility data can be obtained from census data in two ways. The simplest way to obtain an aggregate measure of fertility is to use the total number of children and the number of women of reproductive age. This is called the child-woman ratio. This represents the fertility of women in the past 5 years if children up to 4 years of age are used or the past 10 years if children up to 9 are used. It also reflects mortality of women and especially of children in the recent past. Thus, children who were born in the last few years but who died are not included in the numerator and women who bore some of the children in the recent past but subsequently died are not included in the denominator. Since infant and child mortality is much higher than maternal mortality, child-woman ratios tend to underestimate recent fertility, and the higher the mortality, the greater the degree of underestimation. This problem can be avoided to a large extent if each woman is asked the number of children she has borne in her entire reproductive life, including those currently living and those who have died. Thus, data on the number of children ever born is more useful than child-woman ratio data.

Data from vital registration systems

In addition to census data, information on national populations can also be obtained from registration systems, particularly vital registration systems. The simplest systems just require the registration of births and deaths with data on age of mother or age of the person dying. More complex systems include questions on education, occupation, and more details on circumstances surrounding the event. The data from registration systems provide information on the number of births during a period, usually a year. This data can be used to calculate various birth rates. The simplest rate is the crude birth rate, which is the ratio of the number of births obtained from vital registration to the population size measured by the census or updated from the census. Not all births and deaths are registered in poor countries, so birth and death rates usually need to be corrected by data obtained from a series of cross-checking sample surveys.

In addition to the crude birth rate, vital registration also permits several other kinds of birth rates to be calculated. These other birth rates are usually designed to obtain a measure of fertility that is independent of the age structure of the population. Such procedures are needed because the entire population is not at risk of having a birth, and thus populations with the same fertility behavior will have very different crude birth rates depending on what proportion of the population is of childbearing age.[1]

---

1. The simplest adjustment is to divide the number of births in a year by the number of women of reproductive age. This is the general fertility rate and will, of course, be much larger than the crude birth rate. More precise adjustment for the age of the population can be obtained by looking at age-specific birth rates. These rates represent the ratio of children born to women of a given age in a particular year to the total number of women of that age group. Age-specific rates give several different birth rates for one country. This can cause some confusion in interpreting results, since education may affect not only the total number of births women have, but also the ages at which they have them. Therefore, for some age groups, educated women may actually have higher birth rates even though ultimately they have fewer children. For this reason, it is best to combine age-specific birth rates in some way. The simplest way is to add together all the age-specific rates for each year of reproductive life to determine the total number of births during the lifespan of the average woman. This is the total fertility rate. Slight variations in this process result in gross reproduction and net reproduction rates.

Measurement of fertility and education

Thus, while the data to be reviewed here are simply aggregate data on education and fertility, the comparison of results becomes somewhat complicated because of the variety of ways in which education and fertility are measured in the various studies. Because the results to be discussed are not uniform, it is important to keep the differences of measurement in mind, both with respect to fertility and to education. Enrollment, literacy, and years of schooling may all have different effects on fertility, and thus differences in results might arise from this source. Years of schooling and literacy of adults are the result of previous acquisition of education, and their effect on fertility is delayed. Current enrollment, however, is the result of current educational policy. The impact of current enrollment on fertility is more difficult to measure than that of adult education. Current fertility may be affected by current education policies such as the cost of schooling, but current enrollment levels are also affected by current fertility levels since the higher fertility the less able a society is to afford education.

Literacy and years of school completed may influence fertility differently for several reasons. One important reason is that an additional year of schooling may have a different effect on fertility depending on the level of schooling. For example, small amounts of schooling may increase fertility, but larger amounts will depress it. Safilios–Rothschild has observed that "the negative relationship between fertility and education holds true for all countries but does not operate (at least with an equal intensity) throughout the education continuum. Instead, according to the level of development of each country, this association becomes effective at a different point on the continuum" (Safilios-Rothschild, 1969).[2] In addition, the education of men and women can be expected to affect fertility differently because of their different roles in the reproductive process and the different effects of education on their lives.

In measuring fertility, it is important to distinguish between those

---

2. References are indicated in the text by the author's name and date of publication in parenthesis. Complete reference citations are listed in the sources for each chapter at the end of the book.

measures which control for age and those that do not.[3] The reason for this, of course, is that societies with very high fertility also have large portions of their population under 15 years old who are too young to bear children. Thus, the crude birth rate, which shows births per total population, tends to underestimate the differences in the fertility of adult women. Thus, studies that control for age give a more meaningful measure of the relation. In an attempt to keep these issues of measurement in mind, the various aggregate studies have been cross-classified in Table 1.1 by the method used to measure education and fertility. Some of them represent cross-national studies, and others represent cross-regional studies. The country for which a particular cross-regional study was done is given in parentheses.

Cross-national studies

A large number of cross-national studies have been done using various measures of education and fertility and various methodologies. Table 1.2 summarizes these results.

SIMPLE CORRELATION. The simplest way to study the relation between fertility and education is by simple correlation. Heer (1966), Bogue (1969), Kasarda (1971), Ekanem (1972), Repetto (1974), and Kirk (1971) all have calculated such correlations using different time periods, different measures of education and fertility, and different samples. All of these researchers found strong inverse associations between education and fertility despite the fact that no two studies used the same measures of both education and fertility. The correlations did differ considerably in strength, however, ranging from —0.82 to —0.38.[4] Kirk and Kasarda reported that their results

3. To determine the relation between any two variables (such as the height and weight of an individual), certain other factors (such as age or sex) are held constant. In experimental research this technique is referred to as "controlling" the other factors. It can also be done statistically by techniques which include these other variables as controls.

4. If two variables are so perfectly related that points plotted for these variables would all fall on a straight line, the correlation coefficient would be one. If the variables increase together, the correlation coefficient is positive. If they move in opposite directions, the coefficient is negative. If there is no relation between the variables, the coefficient is zero.

Table 1.1. *Cross-Classification of Aggregate Studies,*
Arranged by the Method Used to Measure Education and Fertility

Measure of education	Measure of fertility					
	Crude birth rate	Children ever born	Births per 1,000 women of reproductive age	Age-specific	Composite of age-specific	Other
Illiteracy	Drakatos (1969) (Greece) Ekanem (1972) Farooq and Tuncer (1974) (F) (Turkey) Friedlander and Silver (1967) Gregory and others (1973) Heller (1976) Kirk (1971) McCabe and Rosenzweig (1976) (F) Russet and others (1964)	Hicks (1974) (F) (Mexico) Lal (1968) (India) McCabe and Rosenzweig (1976) (F) Schultz (1972) (F) (Egypt) Zarate (1967) (Mexico) Cochrane (1978) (F) (Thailand)	Friedlander and Silver (1967)	None	Caldwell (1968) (Ghana) Hicks (1974) (F) (Mexico) Janowitz (1971) (F)	Anker (1975)[a] Bogue (1969)[b] El Badry (1965)[c] (Brazil)[g] Merrick (1974) Schultz (1972) (F) (Egypt)[c] Stycos (1968) (Latin America)[c] Traina and Bontrager (1977) (F) (Costa Rica)[c]
Median years completed	Friedlander and Silver (1967)	None	Friedlander and Silver (1967)	None	None	Ben-Porath (M and F)

(Puerto Rico) Friedlander and Silver (1967)	None	Friedlander and Silver (1967)	Schultz (1972) (M and F) (Taiwan)	Caldwell (1968) (Ghana) Li (1973) (Taiwan)	Schultz (1972) (F) (Egypt)[e]

Percent completing primary intermediate, intermediate, secondary, university

Enrollment:

Freedman and Berelson (1976) World Bank (1974) (F) (India) Kasarda (1971) Schultz (1969) (Puerto Rico)	None	None	None	None	Anker (1975)[a] Kasarda (1971)[e]

Other:

Kirk (1971)[e]	Siever (1976) (Mexico)	Heer (1966)[e] Repetto (1974)[e]	Adelman (1963)[f] Janowitz (1971)[f]	None	

Note: (M) = education of men; (F) = education of women. The country for which a particular cross-regional study was done is given in parentheses.

a. Estimated gross reproduction rate.
b. Fertility measured as percentage of demographic transition completed.
c. Child-woman ratio.
d. Age adjusted births.
e. Newspaper circulation.
f. Index composed of literacy and newspaper circulation.
g. General fertility and marital fertility rate.
Sources: For complete references, see the sources for this chapter at the end of the book.

Table 1.2. *Cross-National Studies, Arranged by Methodology Used*

Study (date published)	Sample	Age control	Income control	Direction of relation
Simple correlation				
Bogue (1969)	80 DC and MD			inverse
Heer (1966)	41 DC and MD			inverse
Ekamen (1974)	32 DC			inverse
Kirk (1971)	25 Latin American			inverse[e]
	17 Asian			inverse[e]
	15 Islamic			inverse[e]
Kasarda (1971)	42 DC and MD (1950–59)			inverse[e]
	60 DC and MD (1960–69)			inverse[e]
	42 DC and MD	x		inverse[e]
	60 DC and MD	x		inverse[e]
Repetto (1974)	64 DC and MD	x		inverse
Multiple regression				
Anker (1975)	69 developing	x		inverse[a]
	29 African	x		inverse[a]
	19 Asian	x		inverse[a]
	21 American	x		inverse[a]
Janowitz (1976)	30 DC	x		inverse[a]
Russet (1964)	38 DC and MD		x	inverse
Ekamen (1974)	32 DC		x	inverse[a]
Gregory (1973)	25 MD		x	inverse[e]
	15 DC		x	inverse[e]
McCabe and Rosenzweig (1976)	48 DC		x	inverse[a]

were statistically significant.[5] None of the others reported on the statistical significance of their results.

MULTIPLE REGRESSION INCLUDING INCOME. Since higher income countries generally have lower fertility, and the education level of a

---

5. Results are considered to be statistically significant (usually meaning significantly different from zero) if the probability that the result could be observed by accident if the true value were zero is very low; that is, the result is probably not just an accidental observation. Calculating the probability of observing a particular value is quite complex and requires a large number of assumptions, but it basically depends on the variability of observations used to calculate the results and the size of the sample.

Table 1.2   (*continued*)

Study (date published)	Sample	Age control	Income control	Direction of relation
Freedman and Berelson (1977)	46 DC		x	inverse
Friedlander and Silver (1967)	all countries		x	inverse[c]
	most developed		x	direct[a]
	middle level		x	inverse[c]
	least developed		x	mixed[a]
	all countries	x	x	inverse[a]
	most developed	x	x	direct[a]
	middle level	x	x	inverse[b]
	least developed	x	x	mixed[a]
McCabe and Rosenzweig (1976)	38 urban DC	x	x	inverse[c]
Janowitz (1976)	54 DC and MD	x	x	inverse[c]
Repetto (1974)	64 DC and MD	x	x	inverse[c]
Heer (1966)	41 DC and MD	x	x	inverse[a]
Adelman (1963)	37 DC	x	x	inverse[c]
	developed	x	x	inverse[b]

Note: DC = developing country; MD = more developed country.
a. Not significant.
b. Significant in less than 50 percent of the cases.
c. Significant or significant in 50 percent or more of the cases.
Sources: For complete references, see the sources for this chapter.

country is also closely related to its income level, the relation between education and fertility will appear to be much stronger than it really is if rich and poor countries are grouped together without considering the association between income and other variables.

Two methods are used for controlling the level of income or development. In most of the studies reviewed, income is controlled by multiple regression with income used along with education and some other explanatory variables. The other way of holding income constant is to separate the observations into groups by level of development. While the multiple regression approach is the most common, several studies actually use both techniques.

Russett and others (1964), Ekamen (1972), McCabe and Rosenzweig (1976), Friedlander and Silver (1967), Gregory and others (1973), and Freedman and Berelson (1976) have all used multiple regression equations relating the crude birth rate to various measures of illiteracy (generally adult illiteracy). All of these researchers have introduced per capita income into the regression equation as well as other variables. All the studies cited except that of Friedlander and Silver show that the larger the proportion of illiterate population, the higher the associated fertility. Friedlander and Silver found that in the most developed and least developed countries, fertility was often lower in the more illiterate countries.

Not all of the inverse results are statistically significant. Gregory and his coauthors found results significant for developed and developing countries taken separately. Friedlander and Silver found significant inverse relations between education and fertility when all countries were grouped together and for countries at middle levels of development, but not for highly or very poorly developed countries. Ekamen and McCabe and Rosenzweig restricted their samples to developing countries, and their findings were not significant. Russett and Freedman and Berelson did not report whether or not their results were statistically significant.

MULTIPLE REGRESSION INCLUDING INCOME OR DEVELOPMENT AND AGE. The studies described above used fertility measures that do not control for the age structure of the population. A number of studies are also available which control for both the level of income or development and for age structure. McCabe and Rosenzweig and Friedlander and Silver cited above use some such measures, as do Repetto (1974), Heer (1966), Adelman (1963), and Janowitz (1971). Of the studies that control for age and income, statistically significant inverse relations were found in all cases for Heer's study and in several cases for Friedlander and Silver. In the latter study, results were significantly inverse only in countries at the middle level of development.

Anker (1965) and Janowitz (1971) analyzed developing countries controlling for age but not for income using multiple regression. They found inverse relations, but these were not statistically significant. Janowitz had found statistically significant results when she had grouped developed and developing countries together and introduced a control for income.

PATTERN OF THE RESULTS. Thus, from the three kinds of studies— simple correlation, regression with an income control, and regression with income and age controls—a pattern emerges. Simple correlation shows the uniform inverse relation frequently cited in the literature. Multiple regression studies that control for income level or age also generally show inverse relations, but these are not all significant. In particular, when developing countries are considered alone, results are usually inverse, but not significant. Friedlander and Silver did find that the countries at the middle level of development had significantly inverse associations. Thus, variations exist in the patterns within developing countries. These patterns persist even when age and income are controlled together.

Thus, inverse results are typical, but these are statistically significant in less than 50 percent of the cases. Part of the reason for this is that the relation of education to fertility appears to differ by level of development. The results also suggest that the relation differs depending on the culture of the country.

EFFECT OF CULTURAL AND REGIONAL DIFFERENCES. The correlations from these studies all show that higher education is associated with lower fertility but that the results differ substantially depending on which countries are grouped together. These differences in how education and fertility are related appear to result in part from cultural differences, as shown by Kirk's results (1971) in which the correlation was —0.55 in Southeast Asia, —0.71 in Latin America, and —0.81 in fifteen Islamic countries. Janowitz also found that the region of the world was a significant factor. Anker found his results to differ by region of the developing world. McCabe and Rosenzweig (1976) found significant results only when they controlled statistically for whether or not a country was Moslem. Thus, regional or cultural factors cannot be ignored. If developing countries of different cultures are thrown together without controlling for cultural differences, then there are lower associations between the variables, since these other factors are so important.

There are several ways of taking these factors into account. Countries could be grouped by region or culture, as was done by Kirk and Anker, or controls could be introduced for region in the regression equation as was done by Janowitz and McCabe and Rosenzweig. Alternatively, geographical units within countries could be used as the unit of analysis. Thus, all different units would come from one country with a more or less homogeneous culture. Although this is only one argument for using geographical aggregates within countries, it is a compelling one. Therefore, studies are described next in which all the data come from one country and in which different geographical regions within a country are used as the units of observation. These will be referred to as cross-regional studies.

Cross-regional studies

There are several reasons why cross-regional studies may prove more enlightening than cross-national studies. First, "this type of analysis . . . is clearly superior to inter-country analyses, since it does not rely on strict assumptions about the qualitative differences existing between individual countries" (Drakatos, 1969). Thus, it is less necessary to attempt to measure such qualitative factors as culture. Second, large numbers of statistical areas within countries can be obtained that are more likely to have similar definitions of variables than might be true with groups of countries. Third, smaller geographical units allow the quantitative characteristics that might affect fertility, such as urbanization and income level, to be measured more precisely. This is particularly true if there are great regional differences in a variable within a country, such as the degree of urbanization.

Thus, cross-regional studies are examined which contain simple correlations between the variables as well as those which use multiple regression to control for other important variables. Only studies of developing countries are covered for two reasons. First, the cross-national studies showed that the relation between education and fertility was much weaker in the most developed and the least developed countries (see evidence by Friedlander and Silver (1967) and Adelman (1963)). Second, from the policy perspective of the World Bank, the less developed countries are of greatest interest. Unfortunately, within the developing world there is a lack of empirical work on Africa. In this case, only one such cross-regional data set was found, and the relevant correlations were not published but had to be calculated for this review. The Middle East, Asia, and Latin America are somewhat better represented. The results of these studies are summarized in Table 1.3.

SIMPLE CORRELATION. Education and fertility at the subregional level have been correlated for many countries, particularly in Latin America. For Brazil, Merrick (1974) reports on the correlations between general and marital fertility and female literacy and child

enrollment for 1950 and 1970. All correlations are significantly negative in both years, but are more negative in 1970 than 1950. Stycos
(1968) reports on simple correlations between literacy and the child-
woman ratio for interregional studies in eleven Latin American countries using data from around 1950. He found correlations were generally inverse, ranging from —0.74 to —0.10; in Bolivia there was
actually higher fertility associated with higher education—a +0.5
correlation. Examining his results, he felt that two factors needed to
be considered: the general level of education and the extent of
urbanization of a country. He found that "when urbanization is held
constant, the literacy-fertility relation remains high primarily in those
countries with the highest educational development—Argentina,
Chile, and Costa Rica." If the areas within each country are divided
into urban and rural areas, inverse relations are more likely to occur
in the urban areas. In Bolivia, Honduras, and Panama, however, the
correlation shows higher fertility associated with higher education
even in the urban areas, that is, positive correlations between the
variables. Looking exclusively at urban areas, Zarate (1967) and
Caldwell (1968) showed inverse correlations between education and
fertility for Mexico and Ghana, respectively.

Stycos's observation is similar to that observed in the cross-national
results. If developed and underdeveloped areas (urban and rural)
are pooled; the results are more likely to be inverse than if they are
analyzed separately. In addition, within countries education and fertility are more likely to be inversely related in the more developed
areas. This is analogous to the finding that education was not inversely
related to fertility in the poorest countries. Therefore, in the re-
mainder of the analysis of the cross-regional data the sample is limited
to those studies which control for urbanization by including it in the
regression equations or by analyzing urban and rural areas separately.

MULTIPLE REGRESSION CONTROLLING FOR URBANIZATION. These results are reported in the second half of Table 1.3. The pattern is
generally inverse, but there are several exceptional cases which show
significantly direct relations. The major exceptions are shown in
Mexico, Taiwan, Israel, Egypt, and Thailand. In Mexico, one study
by Hicks (1974) shows significantly direct relations, although Siever's
results, using somewhat different measurements of education and
fertility, found inverse results which were significant in 1960 but
not in 1970. Since Siever's measure of fertility does not rigorously

Table 1.3. *Cross-Regional Studies, Arranged by Methodology Used*

Study (date published)	Location	Age control	Control for degree of urbanization	Direction of relation
Simple correlation				
Merrick (1974)	Brazil	x	none	inverse[c]
Stycos (1968)	Argentina	x	urban	inverse
		x	rural	inverse
	Bolivia	x	urban	direct[b]
		x	rural	direct
	Chile	x	urban	inverse
		x	rural	inverse
	Colombia	x	x	inverse
	Costa Rica	x	urban	inverse
		x	rural	inverse
	Guatemala	x	urban	inverse
		x	rural	direct
	Honduras	x	urban	direct
		x	rural	inverse
	Mexico	x	urban	inverse
		x	rural	direct
	Nicaragua	x	urban	inverse
		x	rural	direct
	Panama	x	urban	direct
		x	rural	inverse
	Venezuela	x	urban	inverse
		x	rural	direct
Zarate (1977)	Mexico	x	urban	inverse[a]
Caldwell (1968)	Ghana	x	urban	inverse[c]
Multiple regression				
World Bank (1974)	India		x	inverse[c]
Schultz (1969)	Puerto Rico		x	inverse[c]
Drakatos (1969)	Greece	x	x	inverse[c]
Li (1970)	Taiwan	x	cities	inverse[c]
		x	urban towns	inverse[c]
		x	rural towns	inverse[b]
Hicks (1974)	Mexico (states TFR)	x	x	direct[c]
	children ever born (rural)	x	rural	direct[a]

Table 1.3   (*continued*)

Study (date published)	Location	Age control	Control for degree of urbanization	Direction of relation
	children ever born (states)	x	x	direct[a]
Schultz (1972)	Taiwan	x	x (M)	inverse[c]
			x (F)	direct[c]
	(adjusted for multi-collinearity)	x	x (M)	inverse[c]
			x (F)	inverse[c]
Ben-Porath (1973)	Israel	x	(Jewish towns)	
			(M)	direct[a]
			(F)	inverse[c]
		x	(Jewish rural)	
			(M)	inverse[c]
			(F)	inverse[c]
		x	(kibbutzim)	
			(M)	direct[a]
			(F)	direct[a]
		x	(non-Jewish, urban)	
			(M)	direct[c]
			(F)	inverse[c]
Traina and Bontrager (1977)	Costa Rica	x	x	inverse[c]
Siever (1976)	Mexico	x	x	inverse[c]
Schultz (1972)	Egypt—inter- mediate school			
	children under 5	x	x	inverse[b]
	children 5 to 9	x	x	inverse[b]
	—literacy			
	children under 5	x	x	direct[c]
	children 5 to 9	x	x	direct[a]
Cochrane (1978)	Thailand (1960)	x	x	direct[c]
	(1970)	x	x	direct[c]
	change between 1960 and 1970	x	x	inverse[b]

Note: (M) = education of men; (F) = education of women.
a. Not significant.
b. Significant in less than 50 percent of the cases.
c. Significant or significant in more than 50 percent of the cases.
Sources: For complete references, see the sources for this chapter.

control for age structure and since his education variable applies to only those 15 to 29 rather than to the entire group used in the fertility measure, Hicks's atypical results are somewhat more convincing.

In another study of Mexico, Hicks and two coauthors (Del Rio and others, unpublished) found evidence of a change in the education-fertility relation between 1960 and 1970. They maintain that the relation was positive in 1960 and became negative in 1970. At 60 percent literacy the relation became negative. This suggestion of nonlinearity reflects Stycos's observation that the relation is only inverse at higher levels of literacy. Other evidence discussed later also lends credence to this observation.

Schultz's evidence on Egypt (1972) is indicative of another type of nonlinearity in the relation. For equations that measure education by literacy, Schultz found that education and fertility were positively related and that this was significant in several cases. When education was measured as proportion completing intermediate school, the relation was significantly inverse in most cases. Thus, in certain cases the smallest amount of education may be associated with increased fertility, but at higher levels of education, an inverse relation emerges. This possibility will be investigated in the next section.

The studies of Taiwan and Israel that show direct relation in some cases include both the husband's and wife's education in the same equation. Since communities that have above average levels of male education also have above average levels of female education, it is difficult to measure a separate relation for male and female education. Schultz (1972) attributed his mixed results in Taiwan to this factor and attempted to make adjustments by combining data from several different years. After this correction the results for both male and female education were found to be inversely related to fertility.

Ben-Porath (1973) observed different results for male and female education in Israel. In most instances he found female education significantly inversely related to fertility, but male education was significantly inverse in only one out of four cases. In one case male education was significantly positively related to fertility. A direct relation between male education and fertility is one that has been hypothesized by a number of economists. The hypothesis states that male education is positively related to male income, and income may be positively related to fertility, thus male education and fertility might be positively related. This possibility will be explored more fully below, since it has important implications for educational policy.

The last cross-regional evidence of positive relations between education and fertility comes from Thailand (Cochrane, 1978). This study controls for age in measuring fertility and also uses female literacy for women of the ages for which fertility is being measured. This represents the most rigorous age control in measuring the relation using regional data. This evidence shows that in 1960 and 1970 literacy and number of children ever born for women over 30 were positively related and that this relation is significant. For younger women, the results are mixed and not significant. However, in examining the change in number of children ever born between 1960 and 1970, it is clear that the higher the level of literacy in 1960, the greater the fall in fertility between 1960 and 1970. This relation was statistically significant for women in their 30s. This represents a classic case where cross-sectional results are unreliable in predicting changes over time.

PATTERN OF THE RESULTS. Thus, cross-regional studies that control for age structure and urbanization show evidence of (a) a nonlinear relation between education and fertility; (b) stronger inverse relations in urban than rural areas; (c) possible differences in the relation for male and female education; and (d) a stronger inverse relation in the long run, than in cross-sectional studies. Taken together these aggregate data indicate that among the least developed nations, there is some evidence that more education is not associated with lower fertility.

Unfortunately, there are not many cross-regional studies in these countries to examine, since many of the poorest countries lack national statistical systems, such as complete censuses, that could supply the necessary data. However, several sample surveys have been conducted in these countries which, although too localized or too small to allow cross-regional analysis, do lend themselves to the study of individual comparisons of fertility and education.

Individual Data

In this section, the patterns suggested in the cross-regional studies are verified in data comparing individuals. Before summarizing the data, it is necessary to discuss why aggregate and individual relations might differ.

Differences between individual and aggregate relations

First, if the relation is not linear at the individual level, then at the aggregate level the relation will depend on both the individual relation and the distribution of individuals within the group.[6] In this case, policymakers might be misled in following the aggregate relation. Second, education may affect an individual's fertility and also the fertility of others. If such spillovers exist, the aggregate relation would reflect both the individual effects and the external effects. Thus, the aggregate and the individual relation would differ, and policymakers would be more concerned about the total effects than the individual effects. A third reason that individual and aggregate relations may differ is that there may be other factors which independently affect both fertility and education and, if not identified, may lead to spurious correlations. This is true at both the aggregate and the individual levels. If the aggregates are geographical units, however, one such factor that may apply that cannot apply at the individual level is selective migration between areas. The aggregate relation may therefore reflect patterns of location rather than the interaction of the variables. In this case, aggregate relations could be seriously misleading for the purpose of designing policy. Fourth, the

---

6. For example, suppose education and fertility are related as shown below, and three countries have different educational distributions of their population as shown in columns A, B, and C. (Each population has ten people.) Then the aggregate relation would be given by the average education and fertility in each country. These averages are for country A, 0.7 and 6.8, respectively; for country B, 2 and 5; for country C, 2.3 and 5.2. These averages make it appear as if fertility falls when education increases from 0.7 in A to 2 in B and then that fertility rises when education increases from 2 in B to 2.3 in C. This situation does not happen at the individual level and results by chance from the population distributions in each country.

Individual education	Individual fertility	Population at various levels of education for three countries		
		A	B	C
0	8	5	0	0
1	6	3	0	2
2	5	2	10	3
3	5	0	0	5

meaning of the effect of changes in education on fertility is quite different in aggregate and individual data. Thus, the relation between cross-sectional comparisons and observations at different points in time (longitudinal analysis) differs in aggregate and individual data. The question of whether aggregate or individual relations are more reliable for policy depends on the relative importance of these four factors and cannot be determined without further exploration.

Multiple effects of education

At the individual level, education has been measured by literacy status, years of school attended, years of school completed, or the possession of certain levels of certification. It is reasonable to expect these various measures have somewhat different relations to fertility since the effect of education on an individual's fertility acts through multiple channels. Education through literacy gives people access to more sources of information and a wider perspective on their own culture. Education is also a socializing process and inculcates social values. Exposure to these values would depend on the years of schooling. Education is widely believed to provide economic skills, and the level of those skills may depend on the grade level attained. Even if education does not provide such skills, jobs are often rationed on the basis of credentials such as education certificates. These multiple effects of education are shown in Figure 1.1.

Given these numerous ways in which education may affect individual fertility, there is no reason to expect education as measured by years of schooling to be related to fertility in any simple, uniformly

Figure 1.1. *Multiple Effects of Individual Education*

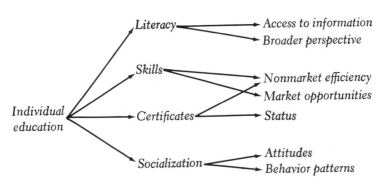

inverse way, much less to expect education as measured by years of schooling to be related linearly to fertility. Therefore, in examining the individual data an attempt will be made to determine not only whether the relation is generally inverse but how uniform or linear it is, what level of education has the maximum effect, and under what circumstances fertility may be higher among the more educated. In addition, the ultimate effects of education may differ for men and women and in different environments. For example, market opportunities for women may be so limited that the effect of education is minimal. This may be particularly true in rural areas.

Spillover effects of an individual's education

As mentioned earlier, education may affect an individual's own fertility but may also have an effect on the fertility of others. For example, the education of one person may give that person access to contraceptive information, but once having such information, it can be passed on to friends. Alternatively, when one person's education increases, their market opportunities improve, but other people's opportunities may be made slightly worse. There are numerous ways in which the education of others or the level of education in the society may affect factors which in turn may affect an individual's fertility. These are shown in Figure 1.2 along with the effects of individual education. If the secondary effects tend to raise the fertility

Figure 1.2. *Effects of Individual and Community Education*

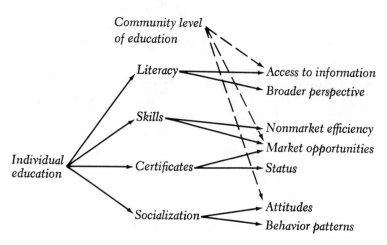

of others, then the aggregate relations would be less inverse than the individual relation. If the secondary effects tend to lower the fertility of others, then the aggregate relation will be more inverse than the individual. Ideally, the effect of both community and individual education on individual fertility should be analyzed simultaneously. A great deal of work is being contemplated that attempts to make this separation.[7] As yet, however, there are few studies which include both the individual and the community levels of education.[8] Therefore, the impact of individual and aggregate education will be studied by examining the relation at the individual level in countries at different levels of literacy. If there is a strong interaction between individual levels and aggregate levels, then the individual relation will differ for countries at different levels of education. But this is only a very crude test of the possible existence of external influences or spillovers.

Spurious correlations

Other problems tend to arise if the units of aggregation are geographic units. In some cases such aggregate relations give a false picture of the individual relation. If geographic units are used, serious biases can arise from migration between units which is selective on the basis of fertility. This is unlikely to arise when the units of aggregation are nations, but smaller regions are more problematic. For example, some cross-regional studies of the United States have used counties as the units of aggregation. This is a serious problem for the analysis of fertility, since many counties around large cities are bedroom communities which tend to attract families that are relatively large and well educated, and smaller families, particularly couples with no children, remain in the inner city which is a dif-

7. A major reason for expecting this is the inclusion of questions on community characteristic in many of the World Fertility Surveys.

8. In a paper by Simmons and de Jong (unpublished) cited in Chapter 6, this has in fact been done in explaining contraceptive knowledge. Anker (1977) has attempted this with some Indian data, but his analysis makes it difficult to determine the direction of effects and so is not reviewed here. David Goldberg (1976) attempted to include both variables in a study of Turkish fertility but included no controls for age, so his study is not included in the review. All three studies tend to show that the community level of education has an effect above and beyond the effect of the individual's own education.

ferent county.[9] This possibility is a self-evident reason for preferring individual rather than aggregate data, particularly when geographic units are small.

Other cases of spurious correlations may arise in both aggregate and individual data. One of these sources of spurious correlation at the aggregate level results from the relation of both variables to the level of development or per capita income. At attempt was made to control for this in analyzing aggregate results.

At the individual level, several factors may be correlated both with fertility and education and thus may cause a spurious correlation. Family income is a frequently cited example. Even more important is age. In most societies the younger generation is better educated than the older generation; thus, an adult's age and education tend to be highly correlated. Fertility is also, of course, highly correlated with age. The older an individual, the larger the number of children ever born. Therefore, if individuals of different ages are compared, a spurious inverse relation between education and fertility will be observed. Therefore, in examining data, only studies that control for age or marital duration will be considered. Limiting the study to those that have age controls eliminates a number of frequently cited studies such as, Miro and Mertens (1968), Safilios-Rothschild (1969), and Rizk (1977).

Policy relevance of differences in aggregate and individual relations

The basic policy question concerning the relation of education to fertility is "what will happen to fertility if education were to increase?" This question can only be addressed empirically at the aggregate level. For individuals, the process of acquiring education and bearing children is such that there is relatively little time in which both activities would be likely to occur. Upper secondary and higher education do take place at ages when many women have children. Thus, it is only at these levels where enrollment in school might have a fairly immediate impact on fertility. But even at these levels the question of how completed fertility would differ if education were increased can be answered only hypothetically, since obvi-

9. These kinds of problems have been studied by sociologists. See W. S. Robinson (1950) and John L. Hammond (1973).

ously individuals cannot relive their lives. Longitudinal data are useful for analyzing the individual relation only in allowing measurement of other variables, such as income, that are specific to the relevant points in time. Such data cannot determine definitely what fertility would have been if the level of education of the individual had been different. At the community level the question may be untestable in practice since a situation cannot be designed in which only education changes and all other factors remain constant. At the aggregate level, however, the question is at least theoretically testable. Thus, at the individual level the question of the effect of a change in education must remain hypothetical. The only conceivable studies that could be done of this kind would be on the effect of adult schooling or nonformal education on attitudes toward, and knowledge of, contraceptive use, but not on the effect on child bearing, which is irreversible. In later chapters evidence of the effect of education on these intervening variables is examined, but at this stage only the relation between the completed or age-adjusted fertility and the education of individuals is considered.

Cross-tabular studies

The simplest way to examine the association between education and fertility at the individual level is to compare the average fertility of the educated with that of the uneducated, that is to say, some education versus no education or the literate versus the illiterate. Eight studies of such comparisons are summarized in Table 1.4.[10] Recalling that only studies that control for age (age-adjusted) are included, the table gives information on the author of the study, the location, type of data used, and the results. The type of data used is designated as either census or survey, and the sample size of each survey is given in parentheses. The results are designated by the characteristics of the individuals reported by the author, by the direction of the

10. Two additional studies use different cutoffs and are thus difficult to compare directly with the others. Caldwell (1968) studied the urban elite of Ghana and found that those who had gone beyond middle school had fertility about 23 percent lower than those with less education. Jaffe and Azumi (1960) examined fertility by work status for Puerto Rican women with less than 5 years of schooling and those with 5 to 9 years. The differences were in the expected direction and ranged from 13 to 20 percent.

Table 1.4. *Cross-Tabular Studies on Age-Adjusted Fertility of the Educated and the Uneducated*

Study (date published)	Location	Illiteracy rate (percent)		Data source[a] (sample size)	Characteristics[b]	Direction of relation	Percent difference between educated and uneducated
Amani (1971)	Iran	(F)	88 (1966)	1971 Tehran (1,338)	(F)	inverse	− 4
Dow (1971)	Sierra Leone	(A)	73 (1968)	1969–70 survey (5,962)	(F) total	inverse	−19
					(F) freetown	inverse	−13
					(F) towns	direct	+ 4
					(F) villages	inverse[c]	−15
Ekamen (1974)	Nigeria	(A)	89 (1952–53)	1971–73 rural (745)	(F)	inverse	− 4
Goldstein (1972)	Thailand	(F)	44 (1960)	1960 census	(F)	inverse	−10
Rule (1963)	India	(F)	87 (1961)	1956 rural (2,380)	(F)	inverse[c]	− 6
					(M)	inverse	− 5
Stycos and Weller (1967)	Turkey	(F)	73 (1965)	1963 urban and rural (2,700)	(F) urban	inverse	−36
					(F) rural	inverse	− 6
Yaukey (1963)	Lebanon	(F)	14 (1971)	1956 urban (613)	(F) Christian	inverse	−20
					(F) Moslem	inverse	−32
World Fertility Survey (1977)	Nepal	(F)	93.8 (1976)	1976 national (5,665)	(F) married 0–5 years	inverse	−20
					(F) married 5–9 years	direct	+18
					(F) married 10–15 years	direct	+10

Note: (F) = education of women; (M) = education of men; (A) = education of adults.
a. Surveys are identified by the date, area studied, and sample size.
b. Relations are specified by the characteristics of samples reported, sex, residence, and employment.
c. Size of one group is too small for meaningful comparison.

34

relation, and by the difference in the fertility between the educated and uneducated expressed as a percentage of the lower fertility level of the two.

There are relatively few studies in Table 1.4, and in some cases the sample sizes and the distribution of education are such that there are too few cases to make meaningful comparisons. In general, the relations are inverse, except for towns in Sierra Leone and for women married 5 to 15 years in Nepal. If more detailed classifications were reported, there would be several other direct relations such as for rural, employed women in Turkey. There is evidence that the higher the illiteracy rate in the country, the smaller the difference in fertility between the educated and the uneducated, but there are too few cases to state this conclusively. For Turkey, the differences are much larger in urban than in rural areas. The uniformity of the inverse relations in Table 1.4 is similar to that observed when simple correlations were examined in cross-national data.

NONLINEAR RELATIONS BETWEEN YEARS OF SCHOOLING AND FERTILITY. One problem with comparing the educated with the uneducated is that all fertility differences among the levels of the educated are suppressed. Therefore, it is impossible to determine if the relation is linear or even uniformly inverse. From a policy perspective, it is quite important to know if education is associated with lower fertility over the entire educational range. Therefore, several studies that show the fertility across several educational groups are examined. These studies are summarized in Table 1.5. Given the suggested relation between the strength of the inverse relation and the aggregate level of literacy in a country, Table 1.5 has been arranged by the aggregate level of female illiteracy at the time of the data collection, if available; otherwise, general illiteracy is used or estimated.

Table 1.5 is quite similar to Table 1.4 except that there is a more detailed description of the relation, as necessitated by the greater number of educational categories used. Thus, the shape of the relation can be identified. If the relation is generally inverse, the number of deviations from a uniform decrease in fertility with increase in education are recorded. In Buenos Aires and urban Thailand in 1969 the relation is irregular, but in the other cases where there are major deviations from an inverse pattern, fertility tends to rise first with education and then decrease. This is labeled as a curvilinear relation in Table 1.5, and the level of education associated with maximum

Table 1.5. Cross-Tabular Studies on the Relation between Age-Adjusted Fertility and Educational Level, by Illiteracy Rate

Study (date published)	Location	Illiteracy rate (percent)	Data source (sample size)	Characteristics	Direction of relation	Number of reversals in relation[a]	Percent difference in fertility between educated and not educated
CELADE[b] (1972)	Buenos Aires	(A) 10	1964 survey (2,136)	(F)	irregular	3	ND
				(M)	irregular	3	ND
CELADE (1972)	San Jose	(A) 14	1964 survey (2,132)	(F)	curvilinear	4 + years	+1
				(M)			ND
Chung (1972)	Korea	(F) 19	1971 (1,883)	(M)	inverse	0	ND
				(F)	inverse	0	−20 to −17
Carelton (1965)	Puerto Rico	(F) 22	1960 census	(F)	inverse	0	−15
CELADE (1972)	Panama City	(F) 25	1964 survey (2,222)	(F)	inverse	1	ND
				(M)	inverse	0	ND
CELADE (1972)	Caracas	(A) 27	1964 survey (2,087)	(F)	inverse	1	−22.9
				(M)	inverse	2	−16.6
Knodel and Prachuabmoh (1973)	Thailand	(F) 29 (urban—18; rural—31.7)	1969 survey (1,064 F; 675 M)	urban (F)	curvilinear	1–3 years	+29
				rural (F)	curvilinear	1–3 years	+29
				urban (M)	irregular	3	+10
				rural (M)	curvilinear	4–6 years	+4
CELADE (1972)	Bogotá	(A) 30.5	1964 survey (2,259)	(F)	inverse	1	−13
				(M)	inverse	2	−35

CELADE (1972)	Quito	(A) 34.6	1964 survey (1,082)	(F)	inverse	2	ND
CELADE (1972)	Guayaquil	(A) 34.6	1964 survey (1,243)	(M)	inverse	0	ND
CELADE (1972)	Mexico City	(F) 35	1964 survey (2,353)	(F)	inverse	0	ND
				(M)	inverse	0	ND
Stycos (1968)	Peru	(A) 39	1960/61 survey (1,078)	(F)	inverse	2	−12.5
				(M)	inverse	0	−33
				(F) Lima	curvilinear	1–2 years	−7
				(F) Chimbote	inverse		+22
				(F) Viru-Huaxlay	inverse	0	−16
Goldstein (1972)	Thailand	(F) 44	1960 census	(F) Bangkok	inverse	1	−8
				(F) other urban	inverse	0	−11
				(F) urban agricultural	inverse	0	−3
				(F) rural non-agricultural	curvilinear	1–2 years	+ 0.1
				(F) rural agricultural	inverse	0	− 8
CELADE (1972)	Rio de Janeiro	(F) 40.6	1964 survey (2,512)	(F)	inverse	1	−22.3
				(M)	inverse	3	−26.6
Gendell and others (1970)	Guatemala	(A) 45.3	1964 census (urban)	(F) domestics	curvilinear	0	+14
				(F) other active	inverse	0	−55
				(F) inactive	inverse		− 8
Palmore (1969)	West Malaysia	(F) 50.4 (urban—42.1; rural—54)	1966-67 (5,467)	(F) metropolitan	inverse		−11
				(F) nonmetro-politan urban	curvilinear	1–5 years	+ 7
Hull and Hull (1977)	Indonesia	(F) 51 (urban—30.2; rural—55.5)	1971 census	(F) rural	curvilinear	1–5 years	+12
				(F) urban	curvilinear	(complete)	+15
				(F) rural	curvilinear	(primary)	+21

(Table continues on the following page)

37

Table 1.5 (continued)

Study (date published)	Location	Illiteracy rate (percent)	Data source (sample size)	Characteristics	Direction of relation	Number of reversals in relation[a]	Percent difference in fertility between educated and not educated
Ewbank (1977)	Tanzania	(F) 85	1967 census	(F)	curvilinear	1–4 years	+12
Srinivasan (1967)	India	(F) 87		(M) rural	curvilinear	6–8 years	+ 1
Ohadike (1969)	Lagos, Nigeria	(A) 89	1964 Lagos survey (596)	(F) urban	inverse	0	− 3
				(M) urban	curvilinear	primary	+ 8
El Badry and Rizk (1967)	Cairo, Egypt	(F) 91	1960	(F) upper Egypt	curvilinear	literate	+12
		(A) 80		(F) lower Egypt—nonurban	curvilinear	literate	+13
				(F) lower Egypt—urban	inverse	0	−14

Note: (F) = education of women; (M) = education of men; (A) = education of adults; ND = no data.
a. Number of reversals in general inverse relations; if the relation is nonlinear, this column reports on the level of education with highest fertility.
b. United Nations Regional Center for Demographic Training and Research in Latin America.
Sources: For complete references, see the sources for this chapter.

Figure 1.3. *Forms of Relation between Education and Fertility: (left) Curvilinear; (right) Uniformly Inverse*

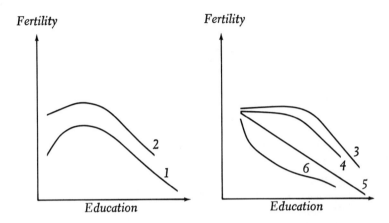

fertility is identified. The last column of Table 1.5 shows the difference in fertility between those with no education and those with a small amount of education. A number of studies do not have enough individuals with no education to make such comparisons meaningful.

Thus, two patterns exist, as shown in Figure 1.3—the curvilinear and the uniformly inverse pattern. There are also variations in the shape of these relations. Stycos (1968) has suggested that the relation tends to be more uniformly inverse in countries with higher levels of education. It is somewhat difficult to examine this hypothesis, however, partially because it is difficult to obtain illiteracy figures for the appropriate time periods. In addition, it is unclear whether it is the education level of the country as a whole or that of the community that matters, or whether it is current illiteracy or that which prevailed when those who have completed childbearing were having their children. Since there are large urban-rural differences in illiteracy, it is difficult to determine which level of literacy is appropriate in cases where results are reported by urban or rural residence. Table 1.6 reports the results in Table 1.5 by the illiteracy level of the country as a whole. The evidence indicates little difference between countries with illiteracy rates under 40 and those between 40 and 60. Countries with illiteracy rates over 60 do show a lower proportion of inverse results, but there are relatively few studies available for those countries.

Table 1.6. *The Relation between Age-Adjusted Fertility and Level of Education, Classified by Illiteracy Rate*

Illiteracy rate (percent)	Direction of relation		Percent of cases that are inverse
	Inverse (number of cases)	Not inverse (number of cases)	
Under 40	13	12	52
40 to 60	8	7	53
Over 60	2	5	29
Total	23	24	49

Note: Figures generated from cross-tabular studies in Table 1.5.

Classifying relations as inverse or not inverse may obscure the fact that there may be a continuum of relation from 1 and 2 to 3 and 4 and so forth, in Figure 1.3. Relations 2 and 3 are remarkably similar, as are 3 and 4. They differ only in what effect the least amount of schooling has on fertility. Therefore, Table 1.7 classifies results by literacy level and by the difference in fertility between those with no education and those with a small amount of education.

Individuals with a small amount of education appear to have higher fertility than those with no education in most cases in countries with illiteracy rates over 60 percent. In countries with illiteracy rates below 40 percent, such individuals tend to have lower fertility than those

Table 1.7. *The Relation between Age-Adjusted Fertility and the Lowest Levels of Education, Classified by Illiteracy Rates*

Illiteracy rate (percent)	Direction of relation			Percent of cases with increases	Percent of cases with large decreases
	Increases in fertility (number of studies)	Decreases below 10 percent (number of cases)	Decreases above 10 percent (number of cases)		
Under 40	6	1	9	38	60
40 to 60	6	4	5	40	33
Over 60	5	1	1	71	14
Total	17	6	15	45	39

Note: Figures generated from cross-tabular studies in Table 1.5.

with no schooling, but not in all cases. Countries with intermediate levels of literacy show intermediate patterns with increases, small decreases, and large decreases associated with small increments in schooling. Thus, there is some reason to believe that the relation shifts from one similar to 1 or 2 in Figure 1.3[11] to one similar to 3 or 4. At the highest literacy levels, an individual relation similar to 6 might be expected.

The studies in Table 1.5 can also be used to determine whether there is a threshold effect in the relation of education and fertility. There are two kinds of thresholds possible—an aggregate and an individual. If there were an aggregate threshold, then education would not reduce fertility unless the aggregate level of education exceeded some particular value. There were insufficient aggregate data for the least literate countries to determine if such an aggregate threshold existed.

Some demographers have spoken of threshold levels of aggregate literacy in a somewhat different sense and have attempted to identify some critical level of literacy that must be obtained before average fertility will begin to fall in the process of demographic transition.[12] Kirk (1971) maintained that in Latin America male literacy must exceed 83 to 87 percent (illiteracy must fall below 17 to 13 percent). This is much higher than the evidence in Table 1.5 indicates. There are two possible reasons for this. First, male literacy generally exceeds female literacy. Second, Kirk found that thresholds for all socioeconomic factors were much higher in Latin America than in Asia. A second aggregate threshold concept was presented in a recent World Bank paper (1974) which showed that crude birth rates did not fall to 40 percent until adult literacy reached 60 percent, and crude births rates as low as 30 percent were associated with adult literacy of 82 percent.

Several writers have maintained that policies to increase education

---

11. Some support for this movement is reflected in the recently published World Fertility Survey for Thailand (1977). For all women and those married less than 20 years, education is uniformly inversely related to fertility. For those married more than 20 years, fertility is higher for those women with 1 to 4 years of education than for those with more or less education.

12. Demographic transition refers to the process whereby societies go from high mortality and fertility, to low mortality and high fertility, and eventually to low mortality and low fertility.

Table 1.8. *Level of Education Associated with Maximum Reduction in Age-Adjusted Fertility, Classified by Illiteracy Rate*

Illiteracy rate (percent)	Completed less than primary (number of cases)	Completed primary (number of cases)	Some high school (number of cases)	Completed high school or above (number of cases)	Percent of cases at maximum effect at less than primary
Under 40	12	6	4	3	48
40 to 60	3	3	1	6	23
Over 60	0	0	1	4	0

Note: Figures generated from cross-tabular studies in Table 1.5.

will not have immediate effects in lower fertility because at the individual level fertility is not reduced until fairly high levels of education are obtained, and it may actually increase with increased schooling at lower levels.[13] The evidence in Table 1.5 shows that fertility decreases with the smallest amount of education in 58 percent of the cases studied. Table 1.6 gives details of the effects of the least amount of schooling. Table 1.8 cross-classifies the results in Table 1.5 by the overall illiteracy level and the level of education that is associated with the maximum decline in fertility. A pattern similar to that observed in Table 1.7 is observed here. Except for those cases which are too irregular for this concept to be meaningful,[14] the lower the overall illiteracy rate, the more likely it is that very minimal levels of schooling are associated with the maximum decreases in fertility.

13. For example, Miro and Mertens (1968) state, "Somewhere at the primary level, especially at the completed primary level, a large decrease in fertility occurs." Jaffe (Jaffe and Azumi, 1960) maintains that it takes 6 to 9 years of schooling before any significant decline in fertility occurs. Such a proposition is occasionally attributed to Stycos. However, a careful reading of Stycos (Stycos and Weller, 1967) indicates that he merely said that the decline of fertility with the level of education accelerated at the end of junior high school. The inverse relation existed at all levels of education. The key to the discussions of individual thresholds in this context would seem to be the words "significant" and "accelerating."
   Serim Timur (1977) has attempted to determine if different threshold patterns exist in different stages of transition. In the countries prior to fertility reduction (Stage I countries), no clear relation was found between education and fertility. In Stage II countries the threshold varies by cultural area.
   14. Rural Malaysian and urban Nigerian women do not show a maximum level. In Buenos Aires this is true for men and women.

Again, this result is qualified by the fact that there are relatively few studies of the most illiterate countries.

Thus, it appears that individual and aggregate thresholds may interact. In this case the best policy for the least literate countries is uncertain. Concentration on educating a few women to levels of secondary schooling will definitely reduce fertility in the short term, but at a fairly high cost. Policies which concentrate on mass literacy will be associated with initially higher individual fertility but will also raise overall literacy, which appears to shift this positive to a neutral or inverse relation in the long run. Unless more is known about why patterns differ, appropriate policy cannot be determined.

DIFFERENCES IN THE EFFECT OF EDUCATION BY THE SEX AND RESIDENCE OF THE INDIVIDUAL. It is possible that the apparent difference in the relation in countries with high and low literacy results from some complicating variables. It may be that as the level of literacy increases in a country, the distribution of education changes in some significant fashion. One very plausible explanation is that equal access to education for women exists only in societies that have achieved fairly

Table 1.9. *The Relation between Age-Adjusted Fertility and the Level of Education, Classified by Group Characteristics*

		Direction of relation		
Group characteristics		Inverse (number of cases)	Not inverse (number of cases)	Percent of cases inverse
Urban	female	15	7	68
	male	4	7	36
	total	19	14	57
Rural	female	2	6	25
	male	0	2	0
	total	2	8	20
Overall	female	17	13	56
	male	4	9	31
	total	21	22	49

Note: Figures generated from cross-tabular studies in Table 1.5.

Table 1.10. *Multiple Regression Studies of Age-Adjusted Fertility and Educational Level, Controlling for Residence and Income*

Study (date published)	Location	Illiteracy rate (percent)	Data source (sample size)	Equation
McCabe and Rosenzwieg (1976)	Puerto Rico	(F) 13.4	1970 census	35–44 working women
Davidson (1973)	Caracas	(G) 27	1963–64, CELADE (2,087)	20–24 25–29 30–34 35–39
Encarnación (1974)	Philippines	(G) 28	1968 National Fertility Survey (used 3,629 single family households)	total urban rural lower income upper income
Rosenzweig (1976)	Philippines	(G) 28	1968 National Fertility Survey (1,830)	35–39
Kogut (1974)	Brazil	(G) 29	1960 census	northeast south east
Iutaka (1971)	Brazil	—	1959–60 urban survey (1,280)	total urban natives urban migrants
Chernichovsky (1976)	Brazil	—	rural (170)	mortality control no mortality control
Davidson (1973)	Mexico City	(F) 35	1963–64, CELADE (2,353)	20–24 25–29 30–34 35–39
Khan and Sirageldin (1975)	Pakistan	(G) 61	1968–69 survey 35–49 want no more (2,910)	total urban rural

Education		Income		Other significant variables
Sign	*Measurement*	*Sign*	*Measurement*	
(F) —	years completed	+	male wage	predicted wage of males and females
(F) —		—		age of marriage
(F) —		—[a]	husband's income	
(F) —[a]	years completed	—		age of marriage; desired family size
(F) —		—		
(F) +		—		
(F) —		—	family income	
(F) +[a]	years completed	+		age of and duration of marriage
(F) +[a]		+[a]		
(F) —[a]		—		
(F) —[a]	years of schooling	—	predicted income of husband	age of marriage / infant mortality / wage of children
(M) +		—		
(F) —[a]		—		
(M) —[a]		—		locale; age; duration of marriage
(F) —[a]	years of schooling	—	household income	
(M) —[a]		—[a]		
(F) —[a]		—[a]		locale; age; duration of marriage; religion
(M) —[a]		—		
(M) +[a]		—[a]		age; age at marriage;
(M) +	years	—	social status	city, size; color
(M) —		—[a]		
(F) —	years	+[a]		age; age at marriage;
(M) —[a]	literacy		land owned or cultivated	extended family
(F) —	years	+[a]		
(M) —	literacy			
(F) —		—		age at marriage
(F) —		—	husband's occupation	age and work status
(F) —	years completed	—		age at marriage
(F) —		0		age at marriage
(F) —[a]	literacy	—		
(M) +	years	—		education desired for child; child deaths; family planning
(F) —[a]	literacy	—	family income	
(M) +	years	—		
(F) —	literacy	+		
(M) +	years	+		

(Table continues on the following page)

Table 1.10   (*continued*)

Study (*date published*)	Location	Illiteracy rate (*percent*)	Date source (*sample size*)	Equation
Knowles and Anker (1975)	Kenya	(G) 70	1974 survey (1,074)	all women
Kelley (1976)	Kenya	—	401 urban nuclear households	all women
Chernichovsky (1976)	India	(G) 71	rural survey (212)	all women
Kocher (1977)	Tanzania	(G) 85	1973 survey northeastern region (800)	20–29 30–39
Cochrane and others (1977)	Nepal	(F) 97.4	1976 rural (122)	all women

high male literacy. Thus, if female education rather than male education is critical for reducing fertility, then the inverse relation would only emerge once women became educated. The cross-sectional data suggest that the relation of education to fertility did differ for men and women. The studies cited in Table 1.5 can be used to test this possibility.

Another possibility is that literacy level and urbanization are highly

Education		Income		Other significant variables
Sign	Measurement	Sign	Measurement	
(F) +	years	+	household income	land owned; urban residence; years married
(F) +	primary		earned	
(M) +	primary	+[a]	household	age of wife
(F) −[a]	secondary		income	
(M) +	secondary			
(F) +	literacy		income from	mother's age; age at
(M) +	years	+[a]	agriculture and other occupation	marriage; number of child deaths
(F) −[a]		−	household	building quality index; no variable significant in
(M) −		+	crop production	demand; equation; all significant in supply
(M) +	years	−	imputed farm income plus	
(M) +[a]	literacy	−	other income	
(M) +[a]	literacy score	−	per household	
(M) +[a]	numeracy	−	member; land area worked	duration of marriage
(M) +	picture vocabulary	−	per capita	
(M) +	induction of classes	−	has positive coefficient	

Note: (F) = education of women; (M) = education of men.
a. Statistically significant.
Sources: For complete references, see the sources for this chapter.

correlated. Thus if, as suggested earlier, education is more negatively related in urban than in rural areas, then the impact of education in the least literate countries may just reflect its impact in rural areas. Thus, the different relation between fertility and the education of males and females in urban and rural areas needs to be explored further.

Table 1.9 classified results by whether they were reported for urban

or rural areas,[15] for males or females, and whether the results were inverse or not. Studies were classified as inverse if they appeared inverse
with, at most, one deviation from the uniformly inverse patterns.[16]
The results in Table 1.9 show that: (a) females show inverse relations
with greater relative frequency than males; (b) urban areas are
more likely to show inverse relations than rural areas; and (c) these
patterns are maintained in sex-resident subgroupings, that is, urban
females show more inverse relations than rural females, and so forth.
The overall proportion of inverse relations of 49 percent then depends
on the distribution of studies over subgroups. Unfortunately, there
are really not enough studies in rural areas, particularly among rural
males, to say that the above pattern is conclusive.

Multiple regression studies

Another reason why education may not be inversely related to
fertility, particularly in the least literate countries, is that all individuals do not have an equal chance of acquiring education. In all
societies the wealthier have a higher probability of acquiring schooling. This is particularly true for societies that are too poor to provide
public education. In addition, education may enable individuals to
earn higher incomes. Thus, since many economists have hypothesized
that income may be positively related to fertility, it is desirable to
determine the relation between education and fertility controlling for
income. However, it is very confusing to control for age, income, and
urbanization in cross-tabular studies, and thus little such analysis
has been done.

There are, however, several multiple regression studies for developing countries that examine the relation between education and
fertility, controlling for age, urban-rural residence, and income (or
husband's occupation in several cases). Table 1.10 summarizes a
number of such studies, giving the identification of the study, the

15. Three studies reported results for national population groups, without
distinguishing between urban and rural subgroups: Tanzania, Korea, and Puerto
Rico.
16. If only perfectly uniform relations are classified as inverse, the numbers in
the cells of Table 1.9 change, as does the overall proportion of inverse relations
(only 35 percent are uniformly inverse). However, the patterns do not change:
urban and female groups are more likely to show inverse relations than rural and
male groups.

Table 1.11. *The Relation between Age-Adjusted Fertility and Level of Education, Classified by Illiteracy Rate*

	Direction of relation		
Illiteracy rate (percent)	*Inverse (number of cases)*	*Direct (number of cases)*	*Percent of cases inverse*
Under 40	23	6	79
Over 60	5	15	25

Note: Figures generated from multiple regression studies in Table 1.10.

illiteracy level of the country, the data source, and the results. The results are reported in considerable detail. Since most studies report several regression equations, the separate equations are identified, and the results are reported in each case for the sign and significance of education and income in the equation. In addition, other variables that were significant in the regression equation are identified. In summarizing the results, each equation is treated as a separate case. This gives a somewhat unbalanced weight to the various studies, but the procedure is necessary because of the lack of consistency in the results in some studies which vary depending on the specification of the equation.

The results can be compared by level of illiteracy as shown in Table 1.11. There are no countries at the middle levels of literacy for which multiple regression studies were available, but the table shows that inverse relations between education and fertility are less likely in countries with high levels of illiteracy even when income is controlled. This confirms the pattern observed in the cross-tabular studies. Thus, the difference in the relation between highly literate and illiterate countries does not appear to be simply a by-product of the association between income and schooling.

The differences in the relation between male and female education and in urban and rural areas may also be altered by controlling for income. In Table 1.12 the results of Table 1.10 are cross-classified by urban-rural residence, male-female education, and the direction of the relations observed. This table is quite similar to Table 1.9 with which it can be directly compared.

In Table 1.12 it is obvious that female education is more likely to be inversely related to fertility than male education as in the cross-

Table 1.12. *The Relation between Age-Adjusted Fertility and the Level of Education, Classified by Group Characteristics*

		Direction of relation		
Group characteristics		Inverse (number of cases)	Direct (number of cases)	Percent of cases inverse
Urban	female	11	1	92
	male	1	5	17
Rural	female	4	2	67
	male	3	8	27
National	female	7	3	70
	male	3	2	60
Total	female	22	6	79
	male	7	15	32

Note: Figures generated from multiple regression studies in Table 1.10.

tabular studies. In addition, females in urban areas are more likely to show inverse relations than in rural areas. The percentage of inverse relations for female education in urban and rural areas and overall are greater in the multiple regression studies where income is controlled than in the cross-tabular studies (79 versus 56 percent).

Male education is less well studied, and the results are perhaps distorted to some extent by the six different equations for male education in the small Nepalese sample. In the multiple regression studies only 32 percent of the cases show male education to be inversely related to fertility even when income is controlled. This is remarkably close to the 30 percent observed for male education in the cross-tabular studies. Thus, income as measured in these studies does not explain why the husband's education is less likely to be inversely related to fertility than female education.

Summary and Conclusions

Studies using aggregate data have shown that many cases exist in which education is not inversely related to fertility, but the relation is more likely to be inverse in urban than rural areas and in middle level than extremely poor countries. Studies using individual data show that at the lowest levels of aggregate literacy, individuals with

THE EMPIRICAL RELATION 51

a small amount of education often have higher fertility than those with no education. This suggests an interaction between the aggregate level of education and the individual level of fertility.

Pattern of results

Studies using aggregate data also show that education and fertility are more likely to be inversely related in urban than in rural areas and that the relation may differ for male and female education. Both cross-tabular and multiple regression studies of individuals confirm the above observations with respect to urban-rural differences in the relation. Cross-tabular studies of individuals show that the education of women is more likely to be inversely related to fertility than is that of men. The multiple regression results indicate that if income is controlled, the education of women and fertility are even more likely to be inversely related than otherwise. This is not the case for male education.

Scarcity of data

Thus, education is not inversely related to fertility in all cases. The reason for the different effects of education in different environments must be assessed before determining the policy implications of this pattern. One reason for uncertainty about the association of education with fertility is the scarcity of studies in the least literate countries, in rural areas, and among males in all areas. In addition, not only are there fewer studies in the least literate countries, but the existing studies are based to a greater extent on very small samples.

There are undoubtedly other studies that have been done and are being done in the most illiterate countries and in rural areas. The acquisition of these studies and the execution of other studies would help determine the validity of the patterns observed in this chapter. However, replication of studies similar to those done here will not be sufficient to determine the relation of education and fertility. Such determination requires a more detailed knowledge of how education acts through other variables to alter fertility.

An analogous but simpler problem exists when determining the relation between a decrease in the price of a commodity and the quantity of that commodity demanded. The paradox of Giffen goods[17]

17. A Giffen good is a commodity whose quantity demanded tends to decline when its price falls.

can be understood only if the effect of price declines is analyzed through their effect on both real income and relative prices. Unfortunately, actual fertility is more complex, involving demand and supply factors as well as the regulation of excess supply. In the next chapter a model of fertility determination is developed to show the multiple channels through which education can act.

Effect of intervening variables

The explanation of the apparently different effects of education on fertility in different environments and between men and women can be understood only if the complexity of the factors involved in determining fertility and the relation of these factors to education is understood. Some insight into which factors should be studied can be obtained by looking at which variables proved significant in the regression equations in Table 1.10. The most striking variable is that of age at marriage. Infant mortality and family planning appear to be significant in several cases. Desired family size, aspirations for children, and child wages also appear to be significant as well as demographic factors such as religion and race.

To properly interpret the regression results, it is important to know the theoretical and empirical relation between these other intervening variables and education. To properly understand the effect of education on actual fertility, it is important to realize that education affects fertility only indirectly by affecting people's opportunities through their incomes, their health, and their ability to control their lives as well as how they evaluate the various options available to them. Thus, education should be closely related to a number of other variables which are closely related to fertility.

As more of these intervening variables are entered into regression equations along with education, the effect of education will appear more diluted. Thus, simple multiple regression equations such as those reported in Table 1.10 may be misleading if education does, in fact, act through these other variables. A more complete understanding of the relation would require linking the many effects of education with the many determinants of fertility. A model of fertility determination is discussed next, and the empirical relation of education to the variables that tend to affect fertility more directly are discussed in detail in Chapters 3, 4, and 5.

2

•●•●•

The Theoretical Determinants
of Fertility

The review of empirical findings revealed that education does not have a uniformly inverse relation with fertility. At the individual and the community level it appears that at the lowest levels of schooling, education is associated with an increase in fertility. In this chapter a model of fertility determination is developed that generates the hypothesis that the positive association results primarily from the effects of education on the biological supply of children, which is determined by health and adherence to traditional sexual taboos.

Easterlin's Model of Fertility Determination

This model of fertility determination is an elaboration of a conceptually simple but extremely powerful model of fertility determination created by Richard Easterlin (Easterlin and others, 1976). His model uses three concepts of fertility: natural fertility, desired fertility, and optimal fertility. "Natural fertility, is the number of births a family believes it would have if it made no deliberate at-tempts to influence its fertility." It depends on the health and sexual behavior. Desired fertility is the number of births desired if the cost of fertility control were zero. The optimal solution fertility or actual fertility results from maximizing utility, given the budget constraint and household technology (including real contraceptive technology and its economic and noneconomic cost).

In the poorest countries poor health, poor nutrition, high mor-tality, and sexual taboos cause desired fertility to exceed natural fertility, and thus actual fertility is determined by conditions of health and traditional sexual behavior. As development proceeds, natural fertility increases, and desired fertility falls. During part of this period actual fertility rises. This explains the increases in fertility that are often observed before demographic transition. Initially, the resulting excess of actual over desired births is too small to overcome the cost of controlling fertility. However, as natural and desired fer-tility diverge or as the cost of fertility reduction decreases, some at-tempt is made to regulate fertility, and the optimal birth solution begins to fall below natural fertility. As contraceptive cost approaches

Figure 2.1. *Easterlin's Model of Fertility Determination*

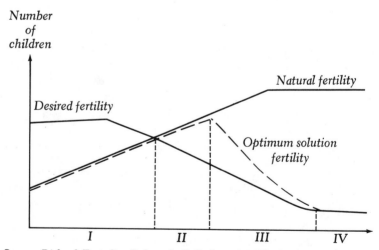

Source: Richard Easterlin, Robert A. Pollack, and Michael L. Wachter, "To-ward a More General Economic Model of Fertility Determination: Endogenous Preference and Natural Fertility" (presented at the National Bureau of Economic Research Conference on Economic and Demographic Change in Less Developed Countries, September 30–October 2, 1976, Philadelphia, processed).

zero, the optimal solution (actual fertility) will approach desired fertility. This scenario is shown in Figure 2.1.

Areas I, II, III, and IV in Figure 2.1 can apply either to time periods or to individuals within a society. Different groups within a society would be located in different parts of the diagram. For this particular study, the position of people with different levels of education is of interest. The results discussed above seem to fit in with the hypothetical fertility differences by socioeconomic groups put forth by Easterlin and his coauthors. In the earlier stage, fertility is higher for those of higher status, and in the later stage, it is lower.

Thus, it is hypothesized that education tends to increase the biological supply of children. Education also reduces desired family size and the cost of regulating fertility. Thus, education initially increases fertility for a society as a whole and for individuals with certain levels of education. Eventually, however, more education results in lower fertility. Male and female education may affect fertility differently because of their different effects on the three main elements determining actual fertility. To determine if this is in fact the case, a complex model of the effect of education on the determinants of desired family size, natural fertility, and fertility regulation is developed below.

Direct, Indirect, and Joint Effects of Education on Fertility

Several people have divided these effects of education on fertility into direct, indirect, and joint effects. The distinction between direct and indirect effects is unclear, however, perhaps because it is difficult to conceive of how education by itself can alter fertility without acting through either biological or behavioral variables (Carelton, 1976; Holsinger and Kasarda, 1976). Therefore, for this discussion, only the indirect effects of education will be considered. Limited attention will also be given to joint or interaction effects such as the effects of education that only emerge under certain circumstances. Evidence cited earlier indicates that individual education may interact with urban residence and the community level of education in such a way.

This indirect approach has several disadvantages, however. It involves a much more detailed examination of materials than a simple examination of the relation between education and completed fertility. In addition, a model must be developed relating the intervening variables to fertility. Given the tenuous nature of the model, it will be difficult to make very concrete judgments about the relative importance of the various ways in which education affects fertility, but the direction of the relations can be established in most cases.

The model of fertility determination described below attempts to identify and to relate schematically the important variables that determine the completed fertility of a married couple.[1] The empirical validity of this model is not estimated, but references are given to support the plausibility of the relations. The major purpose of this model is to identify variables that affect fertility and that may in turn be affected by education. After the model is developed, the theoretical relations between education and these intermediate variables are discussed. In Chapters 3, 4, and 5 empirical evidence on the relation of education to these intervening variables is reviewed.

The Schematic Model of Fertility Determination

In the schematic presentation of fertility the acquisition of an additional child, given the current number of surviving children,[2] is determined by demand factors (current family size and the spouses' desired family sizes); supply factors (fecundity, age at marriage, and infant-child mortality); and the regulation of supply (knowledge of and use of contraception and sterilization). This approach is somewhat similar to that discussed or recommended by Namboodiri (1972), Repetto (1976), Easterlin (1976), and Haas (1974). This approach differs, however, from the work of many economists in that (a) it emphasizes biological supply as well as demand factors, (b)

---

1. With modifications, this model can be used to describe fertility outside marriage. However, such fertility is much less amenable to a decisionmaking framework.

2. This model is based on acquiring surviving children which depends on births and their survival.

it focuses on the decision to add a child rather than on the total demand for children, (c) it explicitly incorporates the separate preferences of husbands and wives and their interactions, (d) it ignores the fact that many of the variables are determined simultaneously with the demand for children in a life-time planning context,[3] and (e) it lacks a formal model structure. However, there are good reasons for this somewhat atypical approach.[4]

Biological supply

The role of biological supply and the regulation of supply in fertility determination have received more attention in recent research for two reasons. First, in his seminal article on the economic model of fertility, Easterlin (1969) emphasized the importance of biological supply factors. Subsequently, in modeling demographic transition and the situations of developing countries, he has stressed that there are countries in which such biological supply constraints dominate and societies—"perfect contraceptive societies—" in which demand factors dominate as well as a continuum in between (1975; 1976). Easterlin's point is that supply factors may be more important in developing than in developed countries. Second, the new home economists have begun to use economic analysis to examine fertility regulation. This can be seen in studies by Michael (1973), Michael and Willis (1976), and Heckman and Willis (1976). However, these economists have yet to integrate their models of contraceptive behavior with the determination of the demand for children, perhaps because their supply models focus on short-term fertility decisions, and their demand models focus on lifetime decisions. Integration on a level that incorporates fertility regulation may only be possible in analyzing the decision to add a child.

---

3. For example, if the decisionmaking context is completed family size, then investments in education by individuals, labor participation, age of marriage, and fertility can be viewed as being jointly determined. If the decisionmaking context is that of adding a child, decisions about the age of marriage, and parental investment in their own education have already been made in the past. Only the current labor participation of the wife will be discussed in such a simultaneous context.

4. In addition to the following discussion, see Boone Turchi (1975) for a discussion of the first three points.

Sequential decisionmaking

The addition of a birth is more amenable to economic analysis than is total family size for several reasons. First, as stated above, it is much easier to integrate contraceptive strategy in such a framework. Second, it seems reasonable to assume that more rational decision-making is involved in deciding to add a child after several children are already born than in deciding on desired family size before the arrival of children. This seems to be true because of the uncertainties involved in producing children as well as those related to economic circumstances and the noneconomic pressures to have some minimal number of children.[5] In addition, this approach is advantageous because the model can be used recursively to determine completed family size, since the direction of the relations between the variables and total fertility and between the variables and the decision to add another child should be identical.[6]

Inclusion of husbands and wives

The separate treatment of husbands and wives and the explicit examination of their interaction seems to be advisable on theoretical and practical grounds. On theoretical grounds, much work on the demand for children has focused on the family's demand for children. Unfortunately, such models presuppose a family utility function. This is a very problematic concept, since it ignores differences in the preferences of the various family members and their different shares in household resources. (See Galbraith (1973), Samuelson (1956), and Nerlove (1974).) A major problem with this concept is how the husband's and wife's preferences are to be incorporated if they are

5. Some evidence exists that economic factors tend to be more important in family size decisions after some minimal family size is achieved. See R. Freedman and L. Coombs (1974) and Eva Mueller (1972).

6. Since most of the existing empirical research has been done on total fertility rather than the decision to add a child, this model is useful for predicting the direction of the relations in such data while providing a more coherent explanation of fertility determination than the standard static model.

not identical. By recognizing separate preferences and interaction between spouses, some of these problems are handled explicitly. In addition, since supply regulation is included in the model and since evidence exists on the importance of the interaction between husband and wife in successful fertility regulation, interaction should be explicitly introduced. On the policy level, separate treatment of husbands and wives is necessary if the different effects of male and female education are to be examined.

Limitations of the model

The logic of the sequential model seems sound. In this approach, there are substantially fewer simultaneously determined variables than there would be in a model of the determinants of lifetime fertility. Only in a model of lifetime fertility determination must the simultaneous nature of the age of marriage, parental education, and fertility decisions be considered. In the incremental model, only the participation of the wife in the labor force would appear to be simultaneously considered in the decision to add a child. For this reason, participation in the labor force itself is not considered an explanatory variable in the model. Wages of women and the compatibility of child care and market work are considered major determinants of both female participation in the labor force and fertility.

The model developed here differs from most economic models because of its lack of formal modeling and the broad range of variables incorporated. It seemed impossible to incorporate such a range of variables in a mathematical model of family decisionmaking, and it seemed more important to include them all than to have a mathematical model.[7] Thus the model developed here seems to be closer to certain sociological representations of fertility determination than to the work by economists. However, there is more economic content in the supply-demand orientation than is the case in most sociological work. This model might be compared to the work by Davis and

7. Such modeling would be more useful if some attempt were to be made to test the model. Since no known data set exists to test this model, such a test is not contemplated.

Figure 2.2. Model of the Intervening Variables Determining Fertility

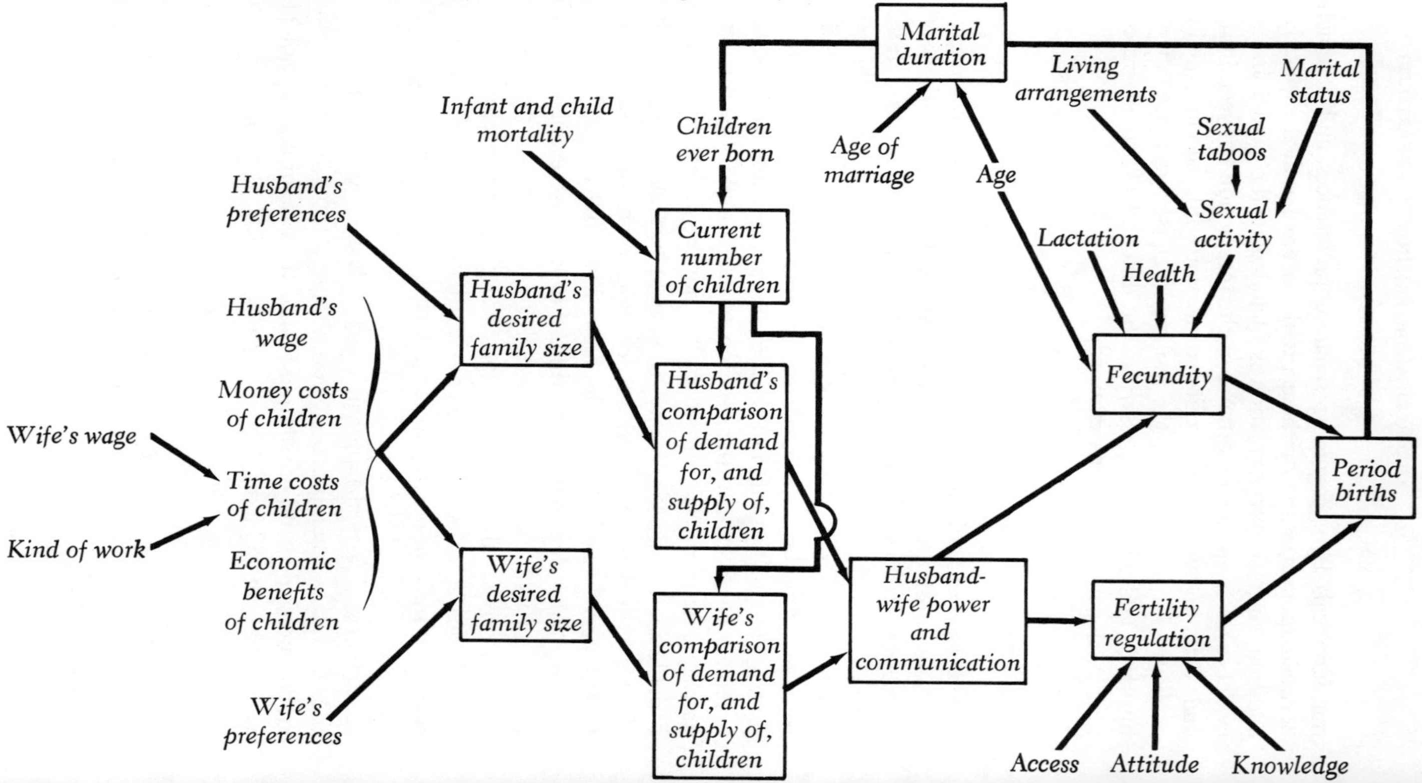

Blake (1956), Rosen and Simmons (1971), Holsinger and Kasarda (1976), Haas (1974), and Namboodiri (1972).

Variables in the model

The schematic representation of fertility determination is presented in Figure 2.2. As mentioned above, this model really has three parts: demand, supply, and supply regulation. Demand factors are presented in the left-hand portion of the diagram. Supply factors operating through current family size and fecundity are presented in the upper-central and right-hand portion of the diagram. Fertility regulation is represented in the lower right-hand portion of the diagram. The proportion of space devoted to various clusters of factors does not represent their relative importance.

THE SUPPLY OF CHILDREN. Supply has a stock and flow component. The potential number of births in any time period depends on what is generally called fecundity or natural fertility. This depends on biological and behavioral factors.[8] Important biological factors include the age and health of the mother, whether lactation is occurring, and the interval since the last birth. The behavioral variables primarily regulate sexual activity. Among the important variables are taboos about sexual intercourse. These variables depend on the marital status of the individual.[9] Sexual activity also depends on the residence of the spouses and the type of living arrangements.[10] The stock of living children in a family is determined by the births in each previous period, the number of periods (generally determined by the duration of marriage), and the mortality of children. The stock of children and demand factors determine whether another child is desired. Fecundity and/or fertility regulation determine whether an additional birth occurs.

8. These are behavioral variables that are not designed to regulate fertility although they may have that effect.

9. Relevant marital circumstances depend on not only whether a person is single, married, divorced or widowed, but also whether it is a legal or consensual union, or a monogamous or polygamous union.

10. In many developing countries men frequently leave their wives for long periods to obtain work. In addition, the practice of living in parental households may also affect sexual activity.

THE DEMAND FOR AN ADDITIONAL CHILD. The demand for an additional child can be considered as either a decision to adjust the stock of children or one which had been made after the marginal cost and benefits of an additional child had been weighed. In the stock-adjustment model, each spouse is assumed to have a desired family size determined by their individual preferences and perceptions of the cost and benefits of children. (These are actually cost-benefit functions and need not be assumed to be constants.) This desired stock of children can then be compared with the actual stock. This approach has most of the disadvantages of the static model of fertility. It is preferable simply to examine the decision to add a child in terms of marginal costs and benefits. Unfortunately, although this latter incremental approach requires fewer constraining assumptions, it is not very useful for organizing a review of the empirical literature because what little evidence does exist on the demand for children has been collected using concepts more closely related to the static concept of demand rather than on the incremental decision to add a child. Although some data has been collected on whether couples desire an additional child, no corresponding work has been done on the marginal, rather than the total, costs and benefits of children. Some data has been collected on the perceived levels of costs and benefits.

Therefore the model used here is the stock-adjustment model rather than a theoretically superior incremental model. The stock-adjustment model is, however, superior to a purely static demand model because it allows for the possibility of altering the desired stock as more information becomes available.

The demand for a stock of children, or a desired size of family, is in some ways more problematic than supply, and it cannot be discussed in the same way as the family's supply of children. Since the husband and wife have desired family sizes which need not coincide,[11] the family's demand for children cannot be defined. Thus the demand for children is determined by examining each spouse's desired family size, which depends on the individual's preferences, perceptions of the costs and benefits of children, and perceptions of the ability to afford children. Neither the preferences nor the per-

---

11. In polygamous marriages the male and female fertility will differ, and the biological supply of children will differ for husbands and wives.

ceptions of the spouses need agree, and so fairly large discrepancies may exist between the desired family sizes of individual spouses.

The ability to afford children depends on family income and wealth as well as on the "price" of children. Income depends on the husband's and wife's wages and labor supply as well as nonlabor income and possibly the income produced by children or other family members. The "price" of children is far more complex. Money expenditures on children are not determined by the market nor completely prescribed by society. While some elements of cost are determined by exogenous factors, such as the price of food, others are determined by parents' aspirations for their children.[12] In addition to monetary cost, children entail the expenditure of time. The time cost of children depends on the amount of time devoted to each child[13] and on the value of that time. Generally in Western societies such time is spent by the mother. In developing societies siblings and extended family members or domestic servants may perform these functions as well. The value of the time devoted to children depends on the alternative uses of time available, on the value of time in those uses, and on the compatibility of those alternative uses with child care. These factors, in turn, depend on the wages of women and children and the kinds of work available. All of these variables thus need to be examined as well as important nonmarket uses of time which may limit the ability of individuals other than the mother to care for children, such as the school attendance of older siblings.

If each spouse has a family size target, it can be compared with current family size to determine the desirability of another birth. It is at this point that child mortality affects demand. Reductions in child

12. This might be identified with the demand for child quality, in the Chicago terminology, but following the lead of Turchi ("Micro-economic Theories of Fertility") and the pragmatic approach of empiricists, these elements of cost will not be separated into the required (price) and discretionary (quality). Parents' aspirations for their children perhaps at best reflect what the economists mean by quality. But such aspirations affect fertility through the perceived cost of children.

13. The amount of time devoted to a child is not fixed in any society but varies enormously depending on wage rates, child care substitutes, aspirations for children and perceptions of the most effective methods for raising children, in particular, the perceived ability to substitute between the mother's time and that of others.

mortality increase the supply of living children. It is also probable that such reductions reduce the demand for additional children.[14]

FERTILITY REGULATION. If another birth is desired and timing factors are ignored, then supply factors predominate. If an additional birth is not desired by one spouse or is not desired at the current time, then there is a potential demand for fertility regulation.[15] Whether a potential demand for fertility regulation leads to actual regulation depends on several intervening variables: (a) which spouse does not wish an additional child, (b) the power of that spouse in making marital decisions, (c) spouses' ability to communicate fertility desires and contraceptive information to each other, (d) the kinds of techniques of fertility regulation available or known to the couple,[16] and (e) access to, and cost of, fertility regulation, including psychological cost of the various techniques.

Direction of the Relations between Intervening Variables and Fertility

The direction of the relation between the variables in Figure 2.2 and the addition of a child are the same as those between such variables and completed fertility.[17] Although scholars do not agree completely on the direction of these relations, there is some general agreement. Column 1 of Table 2.1 summarizes the directions of the hypothesized effects of the variables of the model on fertility. Column

14. It is possible for such reductions to increase the demand for additional children. This latter result is only likely if the cost of children before the average age of child deaths is relatively high. See Cochrane and Cochrane (1974).

15. Strictly speaking, fertility regulation should include stimulation of fertility in the infertile as well as its suppression in the fertile.

16. If the wife wants no more children, but all contraceptive methods are dominated by the husband, fertility is unlikely to be suppressed. The converse is of course also true, so that a wide mix of techniques will increase the number of families practicing contraception.

17. Fertility during a certain period depends on age and time since last birth, which in the long run will not affect completed fertility.

2 gives citations supporting the hypothesized effect.[18] Williams (1976) has recently published a review of the empirical literature that examined many of the variables. The papers by United Nations (1973), McGreevey and Birdsall (1974), and Mason and others (1971) also summarize existing research rather than being original empirical studies.

Ambiguous relations

The two most ambiguous of these relations are the effect of the husband's income and the husband's power in marital decision-making. Although there are theoretical reasons for believing that increases in the husband's income will increase the demand for children and thus completed family size, other things being equal, the empirical evidence does not support this. This probably results from the fact that income is correlated both with wages and with other factors such as preferences, aspirations for children, and access to birth control, and few studies have controlled for these factors (Bean and others, 1977).

The effect of the husband's power is ambiguous on theoretical as well as on empirical grounds. If a man wants more children than his wife, then the greater the husband's power relative to his wife, the greater fertility will be. However, desired family size of each spouse depends on preferences and on perceived costs and benefits. Although wives may bear more of the cost of childbearing, if they have stronger preferences for children, their desired family size may exceed that of their husband's. In such circumstances, increases in the wife's power would not lower fertility. Unfortunately, not enough surveys have collected data on the preferences and power of both husbands and wives to resolve this issue. Weller (1968) found the wife's power reduced fertility among working women in Puerto Rico, and Mitchell (1972) found this to be true among women in Hong Kong. However, both of these are special groups in which a wife's desired family size is likely to be below her husband's. Rosen and Simmons (1971) found that the wife's power decreased desired family size but increased or was increased by actual family size.

---

18. Only published studies have been cited here, and the listing is far from complete.

Table 2.1. *Evidence on the Effect of Intervening Variables on Completed Fertility*

Intervening variable	Direction of relation	Empirical support
Supply factors		
Probability of marriage	+	Schultz (1972), Mazur (1973), Maurer (1973)
Wife's age at marriage	−	McGreevey-Birdsall, Encarnación (1968), Kim and others (1974), Davidson (1973), Yaukey (1972), Palmore and Ariffin (1969)
Health	+	Butz (1976), Baird (1965)
Separate location of spouse	−	Williams (1976)
Joint family living	? (−)	United Nations (1973), Williams (1976)
Legal, monogamous marriage	? (+)	Mason and others (1971) (+), Nerlove and Schultz (1969) (+), Miro and Mertens (1968) (mixed), United Nations (1973) (mixed)
Taboos on sexual activity	−	United Nations (1973) (several studies cited)
Infant and child mortality	+	McGreevey-Birdsall (1974), Snyder (1974), Williams (1976)
Demand factors		
Preferences for children	? (+)	
Husband's wage	?	Simon (1974), Williams (1976)

Relations based on theory

Several of the other relations in Table 2.1 have little or no empirical basis. Some of these are ambiguous because of measurement problems, others have mixed support. In a number of cases, however, the theoretical reasoning is so compelling that, despite lack of data, the signs will have the credibility of those which were established empirically. Among these variables are health, location of spouse, preferences toward children, and knowledge of and attitude toward contraception. The reason for lack of appropriate data differs in each case. Health and preferences are of course difficult to measure. In addition, health, preferences, and knowledge and attitude toward

Table 2.1   (*continued*)

Intervening variable	Direction of relation	Empirical support
Money cost of children	—	Mueller (1972), Bulatao (1975), Arnold and others (1975)
Wife's wage	—	Mason and others (1971) DaVanzo (1972), Snyder (1974), Rosenzweig and Evenson (forthcoming)
Incompatibility of wife's work	—	Goldstein (1972), United Nations (1973), Bindary and others (1973), Williams (1976)
Cost of child care substitutes	—	Cain and Weinenger (1973), McCabe and Rosenzweig (1976)
Economic benefits of children	+	Mueller (1972), Harmon (1970), McGreevey-Birdsall (1974)
Fertility regulation		
Husband's marital power	? (+)	Weller (1968) (+), Mitchell (1972) (+)
Husband-wife communication	—	Mitchell (1972), Michel (1967), Hill and others (1959), Ramakumar and Gopal (1972)
Knowledge of birth control	—	
Attitude toward birth control	—	
Access to birth control	—	Mason and others (1971), Schultz (1972)

Sources: For complete references, see the sources for this chapter.

contraception may all be affected by fertility as well as affecting it. Thus, after-the-fact cross-section research designs that do not measure these variables before childbearing do not provide good evidence of their effect on fertility. Only longitudinal analyses would disentangle these effects. Absence of spouse seems to be a neglected variable that could be collected in the process of obtaining fertility histories.[19] The direction of the effect of all these variables on completed fertility seems to be intuitively obvious even if empirical sup-

19. Williams cites a study by Rele which shows such short-term male migration reduces fertility by one-half a child.

port is lacking. The strength of those relations, however, is much less certain.

Relations with weak empirical support

Several other relations have weak support, such as joint family living, type of marriage, and the cost of child care. In the first instance, there are theoretical reasons for believing there might be a positive or negative effect.[20] Thus its sign is not specified. The evidence on type of marriage is mixed, but there seems to be slightly more evidence suggesting that legal, monogamous marriages have higher fertility than concensual or polygamous marriages, so a tentative positive sign is specified. There is little empirical evidence, but strong theoretical evidence, that increases in the cost of substitutes for the wife's time in child care should reduce fertility. Therefore, a negative relation is assigned here.

Important relations needing more evidence

For several variables the evidence is fairly good, but given the importance of the interaction of these variables with education (to be discussed later), more direct evidence is needed. These are the variables related to the time cost of children, particularly the wife's wage, and the compatibility of market work and child care. The four studies cited here with respect to the wife's wage are less than perfect. The study by Mason and others relies on data from the United States. DaVanzo's study (1972) uses regional aggregate data, and Snyder's study (1974) uses wages for working wives only and sets the wages of nonworking wives equal to zero. Rosenzweig and Evenson (1977) use district wage averages in rural India. The scarcity of data results in part from the fact that many researchers have concentrated on labor force participation and fertility rather than on the wife's wage and fertility. Economists have rejected this approach because the wage could simultaneously affect labor participation and fertility. In addition, family size may affect labor par-

---

20. Joint family living makes child care substitutes more available and may increase fertility. However, the lack of privacy is believed by some, and has been partially confirmed, to reduce sexual activity. In addition there is some evidence that such families feel more constraints on resources. Thus fertility may be limited.

ticipation as well as the converse (Shields, 1977). Another reason for rejecting the labor participation approach is that contradictory evidence exists on whether such an inverse relation with fertility prevails in developing countries where market work may not be incompatible with child rearing. The evidence of incompatibility is based mostly on inferences, since it relies on evidence from broad occupational groupings. Better data on actual or potential wages of women and compatibility of market work and fertility would improve the understanding of both fertility and female labor participation.

The last variable, which should perhaps receive more attention, is access to contraception. The studies cited here use aggregate data on the availability of publicly sponsored family planning, and the evidence is convincing. Where no such programs exist, however, access to contraception may be highly limited by income, which in turn is supposedly affected by education. Thus, some of the differences in fertility across educational groups, particularly the husband's education, may be reduced by providing public family planning. This is an issue that needs to be addressed in discussion of policy.

Relations with strong empirical support

Five variables that appear to have effects on completed fertility are strongly confirmed by empirical evidence. These are the probability of being married, wife's age at marriage, child and infant mortality, the perceived economic benefits of children, and husband-wife communication. The cost of children and the observance of taboos on sexual activity are less well-documented but still convincing.

The perceived costs and benefits of children are being studied increasingly, and the evidence continues to confirm the expected relations. It seems that it is primarily the educational cost of children that dominate parents' thinking (Mueller, 1972). The time cost of children has not been well integrated in these studies, but one of the modules in the World Fertility Survey attempts to correct for this. The economic benefits of children are derived from child labor and old age security. Communication between husband and wife seems to be important for contraceptive use. Some of this evidence was collected when methods related to coitus such as the diaphragm and condom predominated. In those cases cooperation was essential. However, some of the more recent studies indicate that this is also an important variable when more modern methods are used.

Probability of marriage and wife's age of marriage seem to have strong effects, but these are not strictly linear nor are they equally strong in all areas. The nonlinear effect of age of marriage results from the fact that in societies with very early marriages, relatively few women are fertile when they first marry. Thus, increasing the age of marriage from 14 to 16 may have minor impact whereas increasing it from 20 to 22 may have quite a substantial effect.[21] The effect of proportion married on fertility depends on the extent to which extramarital sexual activity and childbearing are accepted or supported by society. Thus, in Moslem countries the proportion married would have a much stronger effect than in the United States.

Child mortality appears to have a biological and a behavioral effect on the number of children ever born. Increasing the proportion of children who survive would tend to diminish the demand for additional births and therefore would tend to initiate behavioral changes. In addition, there is evidence that lactation suppresses ovulation. Therefore, a living infant who is nursing increases the intervals between births.

Having discussed the support for the relation between these intervening variables and completed fertility, the effect of education on these variables and the consequent indirect effects of education on completed fertility through these variables is examined. There is no reason to expect the effect of education to be all in one direction. As explained in Chapter 1, education has multiple effects that affect access to information, market opportunities, nonmarket efficiency, attitudes, behavior patterns, and status. In addition, the relative importance of these effects differ for men and women and also differ depending on the social and economic setting. Therefore, the effect of education on fertility through the intervening variables will be complex and varied.

The Hypothesized Effect of Education on Intervening Variables

In Table 2.2 the direction of the relations between husband's and wife's education and the intervening variables are shown in columns

---

21. If all women under 16 were not yet fertile, increasing the age of marriage from 14 to 16 would not affect fertility.

Table 2.2. *Effect of Education on Fertility through Intervening Variables*

Intervening variable	Effect of education on the intervening variables		Effect of intervening variables on fertility	Effect of education on fertility through intervening variables	
	Male	Female		Male	Female
Supply factors					
Probability of being married	+	−	+	+	−
Wife's age at marriage	?	+	−	?	−
Health	+	+	+	+	+
Separate location of spouse	−	?	−	+	?
Joint family living	−	−	? (−)	? (+)	?
Legal, monogamous marriage	?	+	? (+)	?	? (+)
Taboos on sexual activity	−	−	−	+	+
Infant and child mortality	−	−	+	−	−
Demand factors					
Preferences for children[a]	−	−	? (+)	−	−
Husband's wage	+	0	?	?	0
Money cost of children	+	+	−	−	−
Wife's wage	0	+	−	0	−
Incompatibility of wife's work	0	+	−	0	−
Cost of child care substitutes[b]	0	+	−	0	−
Economic benefits of children	−	−	+	−	−
Fertility regulation					
Husband's marital power	+	−	? (+)	?	?
Husband-wife communication	+	+	−	−	−
Knowledge of birth control	+	+	−	−	−
Attitude toward birth control[a]	+	+	−	−	−
Access to birth control	+	+	−	−	−

a. Depends in part on whether the education is religious or secular.
b. Depends on community level of female education.

1 and 2. The effect of the intervening variable on fertility (from Table 2.1) is given in column 3. The hypothesized multiple effects of education on completed fertility acting through these intervening variables are shown in columns 4 and 5. These latter effects are ob-

tained from combining the effects of intervening variables on fertility shown in Table 2.1 and the effects of education on these variables in columns 1 and 2 of Table 2.2 (that is, multiplying the sign in column 1 or 2 by the sign in column 3).

Several general observations can be derived from Table 2.2. First, columns 1 and 2 show that for many variables, the effect of education differs for men and women. The directions of the effects are the same in only eleven of twenty cases. Columns 4 and 5 show that the education of females is more likely to reduce fertility than is the education of males. In thirteen cases the indirect effect of female education is negative, indicating reduced fertility, but in only eight cases is the impact of male education negative.[22] This provides hypothetical support for the observation that female education reduces fertility more than male education. The evidence supporting the signs of columns 1 and 2 is discussed in Chapters 3, 4, and 5, but first the reasons supporting the hypothesized relations are discussed.

Theoretical support of hypothesized supply relations

The probability of marriage, wife's age at marriage, and type of marriage are all important variables in determining completed fertility. In each case, male and female education appear to affect the variable differently. The age of marriage is the most widely discussed of the three marriage variables, perhaps because it has such a strong negative association with fertility. The wife's age of marriage is affected primarily by the wife's education.[23] Education may affect females' age of marriage in several ways. Education in general raises wage rates and increases access to better jobs, making market work more attractive. Therefore, women may desire to work for some time

22. The ratio of negative to positive impacts for male education is 8 to 5, but for females it is 13 to 4. If husband's income has positive effects on fertility as some believe, the male ratio would only be 8 negative to 6 positive effects.

23. Although male education may affect male's age of marriage, the latter is much less important to fertility than female age of marriage. If there were fixed differences between the age of brides and grooms, male education would increase male's age of marriage and thus would pull up wife's age of marriage, but this seems very uncertain. Thus the effect of male's education on wife's age of marriage is hypothesized to be unknown.

before marriage, thus postponing it. This effect of education would apply throughout all levels of education, but because certificates or degrees are used as screening devices in hiring, this effect may not be equally strong for each increment in years of schooling.

Education may also narrow the range of potential marriage partners and may thus increase the waiting time involved in finding the right suitor. This effect may operate at all levels of education, but the impact may be concentrated at levels of certification or degree levels. Education beyond the primary level may conflict directly with early marriage since married women are generally not enrolled in schools in developing countries. Thus, regardless of the content of secondary or post-secondary education, it will have a very direct effect on the age of marriage in countries which traditionally have low marriage ages. In countries with late marriage ages, this effect of education is unlikely to be important. It would be quite difficult to separate out these different effects of education on the wife's age of marriage, empirically, but such a separation would be quite valuable for designing policy.

Education will affect not only the age of marriage, but the probability of ever marrying. More educated males will be more likely to marry because their incomes will be higher and the choice of partners increased. For females, education increases the alternatives to marriage and reduces the pool of acceptable marriage partners if women must marry men at least as well educated as themselves. These increased alternatives may also increase the probability that a woman will divorce her spouse. These alternatives may also decrease the acceptance of certain forms of marriage such as consensual or polygamous marriages into traditional joint households. Thus, although education of women reduces the probability of being married and thus reduces fertility, it may also increase fertility of those women who do marry because the kinds of marriages they will accept—legal, monogamous, nuclear marriages—are more conducive to higher fertility; but these effects are less certain.[24] If these effects are very

24. For males, the income associated with higher education may permit them the luxury of consensual and/or polygamous marriages. If this were the case, it would tend to raise their own fertility but perhaps to reduce the fertility of their first (legal) wives. The net effect on fertility is fairly uncertain, depending greatly on the kind of values incorporated in the education process. Thus this effect is listed as unknown in Table 2.2.

strong, the effect of education on the fertility of all women may be more negative than its effect on the fertility of married or ever-married women. Since most of the individual studies reviewed in Chapter 1 were limited to married women, the effect of education on overall fertility would tend to be underestimated if education of women reduces the proportion ever marrying.

The other major effects of education on the biological supply of children act through the health of the parents and children and the behavioral variables affecting supply, such as living arrangements and observance of taboos on sexual activity. The biological effects are somewhat clearer. Education would seem to increase the health of parents and children through better knowledge of hygiene and nutrition and better access to modern medicine and adequate food supplies. Although the health of males might be expected to have a smaller effect on fertility than the health of females, ultimately poor health means earlier death of the husband and shorter marriage duration.

The behavioral variables that may affect the supply of births through sexual activity are location of spouse, residence in extended families, and the acceptance of taboos on sexual activity. The practices of living in joint households and of having the husband leave the wife for long periods to work in other areas are associated with low income and low education. Since education, particularly the education of males, tends to reduce these practices, it will tend to increase fertility. In addition, since education changes adherence to traditional patterns of behavior, it will tend to reduce compliance with traditional sexual taboos such as postpartum abstinence and thus will tend to raise fertility.

Therefore, on the supply side, education has positive and negative effects on fertility. The positive effects act through health and the level of sexual activity. The negative effects result primarily from the effect of female education on the age of wife at marriage and the probability of marrying. Education's effect through infant and child mortality is more complex. Its negative effect on completed family size probably results, at least in part, from the reduced demand for additional births. Overall male education is generally associated with increases in the supply of children, but female education has mixed effects on supply.

Theoretical support of hypothesized demand relations

Although education has positive and negative effects on fertility on the supply side, the vast majority of its effects on the demand for children are negative as shown in Table 2.2. The effect of education on demand also depends primarily on the wife's, as opposed to the husband's, education. The least certain effects of education on the demand for children or desired family size are those which act through preferences and the husband's income. While it is quite clear that education is likely to increase the husband's income, it is unclear whether this will increase fertility. However, there is a little uncertainty about the effect of education on the preferences for children. Generally, education reduces such preferences by changing traditional values and increasing awareness of alternative sources of satisfaction. However, the effect of family size preferences, such as ideal family size, on behavior is not well established empirically.

Although the income effects of education on demand are unclear, the cost effects are strongly negative. Education very clearly tends to raise the perceived cost of children and to reduce the economic returns from them. The economic returns from children accrue in the form of child labor and support by children in old age. These costs and benefits can be altered either by changes in external circumstances such as opportunities for child labor or by changes in values on attitudes. Since education results in a shift of occupations from agricultural self-employed to urban employee, child labor is less important within the family, and employment of children outside the family becomes less acceptable as aspirations for the high educational achievement of children increase. These shifts in occupation primarily result from changes in male occupation, but aspirations may be affected by male or female education. The security motive for having children may be affected by male and female education. The more educated generally have better access to capital markets and are more likely to be employees in organizations that provide some form of retirement. In addition, women with job skills need rely less on children for support if their spouse dies.

The money cost of children also depends on the education of both parents. By raising the aspirations for children, education raises the

expenditures that parents make on these children—particularly educational expenditures. The time cost of children is affected primarily
by the education of the wife and of women in general. The higher
the wife's education, the higher her potential wage, and the more
likely it is that a job will be available in the modern sector. Such
jobs have two important characteristics—they are more attractive, and
they are less likely to be compatible with child rearing. Both of these
factors raise the cost of time devoted to child care.[25] In addition to
the effect of the wife's education on her own opportunity cost of
time, female education in general will affect the cost of substitutes
for mother's time in child care. Higher education of adult women
means that many women have alternatives that are better paying
and perhaps more attractive than domestic service. The enrollment
of female children in school makes it difficult for mothers to rely on
their older daughters to care for younger children. This is a possible
source of the interaction between individual fertility and community
education noted in earlier studies. If women in general have very
little education, an educated woman can afford massive child care
substitutes and thus can combine the benefits of education with
high fertility. Once the general level of female education is high, this
is no longer possible because the child care substitutes are in school
themselves or have qualified for higher paid work than child care
service.

Thus, unless a positive effect of male wages on the demand for
children can be established, it is fairly evident that the general impact
of education on the demand for children is negative. This applies to
the education of the wife and to the general level of education of
women. The education of males reduces the perceived economic returns of children and raises the cost by increasing aspirations for
the children.

Theoretical support of hypothesized relation of education and fertility regulation

Education increases the ability to regulate fertility, and thus its
effect on completed fertility is negative for male and female education. It is hypothesized that the wife's education is more important

---

25. The more attractive a job, the higher the satisfaction derived and the higher
the benefits from work.

than the husband's in gaining knowledge and forming attitudes.

Education is hypothesized to increase the knowledge of contraceptive methods, and it would be a more important determinant of knowledge in areas without active public family planning programs. Education is also expected to make people more receptive to new ideas and more likely to approve the use of contraceptives. Since education is also associated with higher income, it is expected to be associated with increased access to contraception and abortion, particularly in areas without widespread public family planning programs.

Education is also hypothesized to affect contraceptive behavior indirectly by altering how spouses make decisions. Increased education is expected to increase discussion between husband and wife. Such discussion is necessary for successful contraception use and also for a consensus on practicing contraception. In addition, the wife is expected to have more responsibility and influence in family decisionmaking if she has more education. The effect of the husband's education on his wife's role in decisionmaking depends largely on the kind of education.

Summary

The most important indirect effects of education would be assumed to be those acting through proportion married or probability of marrying, the age of marriage,[26] infant and child mortality, the perceived cost of children, economic benefit of children, time cost of children (wages of wife, compatibility of wife's work, availability of child care substitutes), communication between husband and wife, and the birth control variables. Health and preferences are more intractable.

However, the effect of education on the ability to regulate fer-

26. Duza and Baldwin (1974) give some impressive evidence on the importance of marital behavior in fertility declines. This evidence indirectly supports the emphasis on such behavior in this model of fertility determination. In Korea between 1960 and 1970, changes in marital structure explained 35 percent of the change in fertility. In West Malaysia it explained 67 percent, in Taiwan it explained 23 percent. In the Philippines marital structure accounted for two-thirds of the reduction. These figures were cited from Cho and Rutherford (1973). R. Freedman and others (1970) attribute 10 of the 40 percent decline in Hong Kong's crude birth rate (1961–68) to delayed marriage.

tility is only relevant if the potential supply of children exceeds the demand. There may be certain situations where this does not occur, and this may explain the lack of a relation between education and fertility in those situations. In certain situations where the demand for children exceeds the supply, education may be associated with a greater biological supply of children (as explained above) without having any affect on the demand for children or even occasionally increasing it.

It is evident that a large part of the negative effect of female education on fertility is believed to result from the employment opportunities for women—higher wages, greater attractiveness of jobs available, and the incompatibility of childbearing and market work. If for some reason these factors are not present, then a large part of the effect of female education on fertility will not operate. It seems more likely that these market effects of female education will emerge in urban rather than rural areas. Modern sector, high-status jobs are rare in rural areas, and if female education increases status, educated women may in fact be less likely to work at available jobs than uneducated women (Goldstein, 1972). This may explain part of the interaction of education and urban residence. It may be that the conditions which stimulate all the negative effects of education on fertility occur only in urban areas. Unfortunately, the relevant kind of information on female market alternatives is fairly scarce. This study attempts to gather what evidence is available on the relation between female education and job opportunities, as well as other relations, but much more empirical research on this topic is needed.

The next chapters establish the extent to which education affects intervening variables by examining the empirical evidence on the relation between education and the relevant variable within the model established in Figure 2.2. In some cases the evidence is quite substantial; in other cases, it is nonexistent. In addition, education is related also to some intermediate variables—desired family size and contraceptive use. Education cannot directly affect these variables but acts through the more elementary intervening variables. However, examination of the relations between these intermediate variables and education allows the relative importance of the effect of education through various channels to be judged.

3

•–•••–•

Education and the Biological Supply of Children

As described in the previous chapter, education affects fertility partially through factors determining the supply of children or natural fertility. The effects of education on the age of marriage and the proportion ever marrying are expected to reduce the biological supply of children, but its effects on health of parents and children as well as on certain behavioral factors such as lactation practices and observance of sexual taboos are expected to increase the potential supply of living children. Thus, the net effect of education on the potential supply of children through these factors is impossible to determine theoretically. However, the magnitude of these effects on various supply variables can be determined by surveying the relevant empirical work. The literature on the effects of education on marital behavior and on the other biological and behavioral supply factors is examined below.

Education and Marriage

The proportion married in any group affects the fertility of that group. At the individual level, education may affect the probability of marrying at each age, and thus the age of marriage, as well as the probability of completing one's reproductive life without ever being married.

Effect on the proportion never married

In Chapter 2 the probability of ever being married was hypothesized to be inversely related to education for women and directly related for men. Several studies confirm this pattern for women, but the pattern is not universally valid.

CROSS-NATIONAL PATTERNS. On a cross-national level, Ruth Dixon (1971) has analyzed the proportion of women 40 to 44 who have never been married. She included measures of female literacy as well as the gainful employment of women 20 to 24 along with other explanatory variables. Female literacy was lower in countries with higher female rates of spinsterhood in the Western European and English overseas countries. In Eastern Europe, the Middle East, and Asia, however, the higher the female literacy, the higher the proportion of women not married in the 40 to 44 age group.[1] Female literacy had little effect on the proportion of males ever married in this age group.[2] The proportion of employed females aged 20 to 24 had no relation to the proportion never married, aged 40 to 44 in the West, but there was a high positive correlation in the East.[3] The very different effects of female literacy and female employment on

1. Dixon uses an East-West distinction rather than the more conventional Western-versus-tradition distinction of Hajnal. Dixon's distinction is based on the greater emphasis on individual responsibility and its effect on the feasibility of marriage in the West.
2. In general, female behavior was much better explained by measures of the feasibility and desirability of marriage than was male marriage behavior.
3. Female employment or female literacy were never the most important factors, but they were more important in the East than in the West. In the East, female employment was a more important variable than female literacy.

the proportion of women married in the East and West is part of a general pattern observed by Dixon. In the West, the poorer the country, the higher the proportion never married. In the East, the richer the country, the higher the proportion never married. Dixon hypothesized that this resulted from the differences in the feasibilities of marriage in poor societies which have predominantly nuclear families and in those which have predominantly extended families. If nuclear families are the norm, as in the West, the poorest countries have fewer couples who can afford to set up the nuclear households necessary for marriage.

CROSS-REGIONAL PATTERNS. Since the developing countries are the greatest concern, it is interesting to determine if, for those countries, the Eastern pattern of an inverse relation between education and probability of marriage persists. The studies listed in Table 3.1 give information on Thailand, Chile, Taiwan, and 19th century Russia. The methodology of the studies differs, but generally female educa-

Table 3.1. *Evidence on Education and the Proportion Ever Married*

Study (date published)	Location (type) (sample size)	Method	Direction of relation	
Chojnacka (1976)	Russia, 19th century (cross-regional)	correlation	(M)	inverse
			(F)	inverse
DaVanzo (1972)	Chile (cross-regional)	multiple regression	(F)	legal direct
			(F)	consensual inverse
			(M)	legal inverse
			(M)	consensual direct
		estimated net effect	(F)	direct
			(M)	inverse
Dixon (1971)	(cross-national)	correlation	(F)	East—inverse
			(F)	West—direct
Maurer and others (1973)	Thailand (cross-regional)	multiple regression	(F)	inverse
			(M)	direct
Speare and others (1973)	Taiwan (individual) (3,579)	multiple classification	(F)	inverse

Note: (F) = education of women; (M) = education of men.
Sources: For complete references, see the sources for this chapter.

tion can be said to increase the proportion never marrying except for Chile.

For 19th century Russia, Chojnacka (1976) found that literacy was negatively correlated with proportion married for men and women in urban and rural areas, but the effect was much stronger for women than for men. For Taiwan, Speare and others (1973) found all increases in female education reduced the proportion married even when age, work experience, and residence were controlled.

The other two studies have more complex results. In a cross-regional analysis of Thailand, Maurer and others (1973) found that for women, education decreased the proportion married at all ages. For men, education decreased the proportion married for those under 30 and increased it for those over 30. Thus it increased the proportion eventually marrying. This conforms to the hypothesis specified in columns 1 and 2 of Table 2.1.

DaVanzo (1972) has analyzed the effects of male and female education in a cross-regional study of Chile. Unfortunately, her results cannot be compared directly with those of Thailand since the analysis of marriage in Latin America requires the separate analysis of legal and consensual marriages. Female schooling increases the proportion of females legally married for women in five-year age groups between 15 and 40 and for all women 15 to 49, but the coefficient is not significantly different from zero for women in their 40s. Male education decreases the proportion legally married; the coefficients have somewhat lower values than female education, but for the ordinary least squares equations the coefficients are significant for males under 40. For consensual unions, the results are reversed. For all ages, female education has a significantly negative correlation. For males, the coefficients are positive but are significant only for males 15 to 19. It is quite obvious from DaVanzo's work that education of males and females does have a different impact on marriage behavior. For the purposes of this study, however, an analysis of the percent not married (legally or consensually) would have been more useful. Some information on this can be gained by comparing the size of the coefficients for the legal and consensual unions.[4] Since the coefficient

---

4. Since people must be either not married, legally married, or consensually married, the coefficients must add to zero, since a change of 1 year of schooling can increase the proportion in one group only at the expense of the others. This assumes that the dependent variable has been appropriately constrained.

for female education is a larger absolute number for legal than consensual unions, increases in schooling must increase those legally
married more than it decreases the number consensually married, and
therefore it must reduce the proportion single. For males, education
increases the proportion single at all ages. Both of these results are
contrary to the hypotheses set forth and to the other evidence. The
only likely explanation would seem to be that Chile does not follow
the Eastern pattern, but rather that, as in the West, education increases the probability of marriage for women. The male behavior,
however, is very atypical.

To use education as a way to reduce fertility through lower proportions married, it would be important to identify more specifically
the kinds of countries in which marriage is made more likely by
higher education and the countries where it is made less likely.

Effect on the age of marriage

While little additional evidence of the relation between education
and proportion never married was found, some inferences can be
made from other kinds of studies. Since there is generally a close
positive relation between the proportion of women never married
and female age of marriage,[5] much can be inferred from reviewing
data on the age of marriage. The substantial evidence on the effect
of education on the age of marriage is summarized in Table 3.2.

CROSS-NATIONAL PATTERNS. To gain a general perspective, Dixon's
cross-national study is again useful. Rather than using age at marriage,
Dixon used the proportion unmarried in the 20 to 24 age group. This,
she felt, could reflect the pattern of age of marriage. Again, the effect
of female literacy on proportion married at young ages differs between the East and West. In the West, higher literacy is positively
correlated with the proportion of women and men married, but this
variable is not important in multiple regression. In the East, female
literacy is negatively correlated with the proportion of men and
women married in this age group, and female literacy is the most
important variable in multiple regression analysis for women but not
for men. In the East, but not the West, the proportion of women 20

5. Dixon found a correlation of 0.78 for women but only 0.48 for men. For
Asia where the proportion-never-marrying is generally low, Smith found a correlation of 0.64.

Table 3.2. *Evidence on Education and the Age of Marriage*

Study (date published)	Location (sample size)	Method	Direction of relation
Cross-national			
Dixon (1971)	57 countries	multiple regression	(F) direct[e]
	Western Europe and English overseas	multiple regression	(F) inverse
	eastern Europe, Middle East, Asia	multiple regression	(F) direct[e]
Cross-regional			
Smith (1977)	10 Asian countries (pooled)	correlation	(M) and (F) direct
	10 Asian countries (individually)	correlation	(M) and (F) direct
Cross-tabular—individual data			
Amani (1971)	Iran urban survey (2,000)	cross-tabular	(F) direct
Caldwell (1968)	Ghana urban elite (627)	cross-tabular	(F) direct (M) irregular
Chander and Palan (1977)	West Malaysia WFS (1974) (5,360 households)	cross-tabular	(F) direct
Chung (1972)	Korea 1971 survey (1,933)	cross-tabular	(F) direct[e]
Hawley and Prachuabmoh (1966)	Thailand 1964 survey (1,207)	cross-tabular	(F) irregular
Lapierre–Adamcyk and Burch (1972)	Korea	cross-tabular	(F) urban—direct (F) rural—direct
Mott (1976)	western Nigeria (395)	cross-tabular	(F) direct
Nayar (1974)	India 1961 Kerala	cross-tabular	(F) urban—direct (F) rural—direct

Table 3.2 (*continued*)

Study (date published)	Location (sample size)	Method	Direction of relation
Olusanya (1971)	Nigeria (4,408)	cross-tabular	(F) direct (M) curvilinear
Palmore and Ariffin (1969)	West Malaysia (5,457)	cross-tabular	(F) direct
Stycos (1968)	Peru		
	(699)	cross-tabular	(F) Lima—direct
	(177)	cross-tabular	(F) Chimbote—curvilinear
	(202)	cross-tabular	(F) Viru-Huaylos—direct
Stycos and Weller (1967)	Turkey 1963 survey (2,700)	cross-tabular	(F) urban—direct (F) rural—direct
World Fertility Survey (1977)	Nepal (5,665)	cross-tabular	(F) direct (M) inverse
Yaukey (1963)	Lebanon (613)	cross-tabular	(F) Moslem—direct (F) Christian—no relation
Yaukey and Thorsen (1972)	San Jose (2,132)	cross-tabular	(F) legal—curvilinear (F) consensual—inverse
	Caracas (2,087)	cross-tabular	(F) legal—direct (F) consensual—direct
	Mexico City (2,353)	cross-tabular	(F) legal—direct (F) consensual—direct
	Bogotá (2,259)	cross-tabular	(F) legal—direct (F) consensual—direct
	Rio de Janeiro (2,512)	cross-tabular	(F) legal—direct (F) consensual—direct
Regression—individual data			
9 CELADE cities (1972)	(See table 5) ideal age of marriage	correlation multiple regression	(M and F) direct (F) direct[a] except San Jose and Quito (M) direct[b]

(*Table continues on the following page*)

Table 3.2   (*continued*)

Study (*date published*)	Location (*sample size*)	Method	Direction of relation	
Harmon (1970)	Philippines 1968 survey (7,237)	multiple regression	(F)	direct[c]
Knowles and Anker (1975)	Kenya 1974 survey (1,074)	multiple regression	(F)	direct[c]
Kogut (1974)	Brazil 1960 census	multiple regression	(F) (M)	direct[c] direct
Paydarfar (1975)	Iran ideal age for daughter	correlation		
	(1,062 urban)		(F and M)	urban— direct[c]
	(176 rural)		(F and M)	rural— none
	(146 tribal)		(F and M)	tribal— none

Note: (F) = education of women; (M) = education of men.
a. Statistically significant except in San Jose and Quito.
b. Statistically significant only in Quito.
c. Statistically significant.
Sources: For complete references, see the sources for this chapter.

to 24 employed was important in explaining proportion married at these ages. Thus even though the proportion married at 20 to 24 may not be perfectly correlated with age of marriage, possible East-West differences should be expected, and the East pattern should correspond to the hypotheses about education and age of marriage discussed in the previous section. Since only developing countries are considered, the East pattern should predominate.

The studies listed in Table 3.2 differ greatly in geographical location and methodology. Latin America is best represented in the studies because of the CELADE work. Asia is represented by five countries and Africa by three. The Middle East is represented by Lebanon, Iran, and Turkey. The methodology of these studies ranges from two-category cross-tabulations to multiple regression analysis.

CROSS-TABULAR PATTERNS. The data reported on Iran, Lebanon, and Western Nigeria involve simple comparisons between two educational groups. Mott's study of Western Nigeria (1976) shows that a lower proportion of women 15 to 19 with some education are married than are those with no education, 33 and 70 percent, respectively. Mott and Amani (1971) show that literate women in the city of Isfahan marry on the average a year later than illiterate women. Yaukey (1963) shows that among urban Moslem women in Lebanon, the educated marry a year later than the uneducated, but there is no difference in age of marriage by education among Christian women.[6]

More detailed cross-tabular comparisons are reported in eight studies that present interesting information on the direction and magnitude of the relation. For the most part this evidence shows uniformly positive relations between the education of women and age at marriage. There are three irregularities in these results. For one area of Peru in Stycos' study (1968), and for San Jose in the Yaukey-Thorsen study (1972), the lowest educational group marries later than some other groups. Yaukey and Thorsen found this to be true of both legal and consensual unions in San Jose. In their study of rural Thailand, Hawley and Prachuabmoh (1966) found several irregularities in the relation for various age groups and for the sample as a whole. On the average, those with no education married somewhat later than those with 1 to 4 years of school, but this pattern was not uniform for all age groups.

The two studies which include male education in cross-tabular analysis show irregular results. In Nigeria, Olusanya (1971) found that males with no education marry later than all other men except those who have attended a university. Caldwell (1968) used proportions of males marrying in each age group and found that fewer of the males with middle school had married by 25 and by 30 than those of any other group. However, Caldwell's data are not completely representative, since he studied an elite group in urban Ghana. The data from the Nepal World Fertility Survey (1977) shows that men with some schooling marry a little earlier than males with no schooling. Thus, there is mixed evidence of the relation between male education and age of marriage.

6. Christian women marry on the average two years later than educated Moslem women. It may be that the higher the average age of marriage, the lower the effect of education as hypothesized in Chapter 2.

What can be said about the size of the effect of education on age of marriage? The studies which show a uniform relation between education and age of marriage differ in the categories used, making comparisons difficult. However, two patterns emerge. The least uniformity appears in comparisons between those with no education and those with primary schooling. The two studies of Korea (Chung, 1972; Lapierre-Adamcyk, 1972) show about a 2-year difference in the age of marriage for these groups. The Malaysian World Fertility Survey (1977) shows differences of slightly more than 1 year. The Nepal World Fertility Survey shows a difference of 0.6 years. The Indian study (Nayar, 1974) shows differences of between 0.5 and 0.9 years. This is close to the 0.6 difference found in the Nigerian study. Stycos found differences as low as 0.5 for women who attended only 1 year of school, as large as 1.8 for those who attended 4 years, and slightly larger differences for those who attended 5 or 6 years. However, in Chimbote those who had attended 5 to 6 years had about the same age of marriage as those with no schooling, and those with between 1 and 5 years schooling had lower ages of marriage. Thus, the effect of small amounts of schooling differs greatly from 2 years to less than a year, and in some cases even a lower age of marriage is observed for those with a small amount of schooling.

The difference in age of marriage between primary completion and secondary completion seems to be substantial in all cases. In the five Latin American cities in the Yaukey and Thorsen study and in the two cities for which data exist in Stycos's study of Peru, the difference ranges from 0.7 to 3 years (1.8 years is the unweighed average difference in these seven cities). In Nigeria the difference was 4.5 years. In India, it ranged from 1.3 to 2.8 depending on area, with larger differences in rural areas. The Lapierre-Adamcyk study of Korea shows the difference to be about 1.7 years. The Malaysian World Fertility Survey shows differences of almost 3 years except for women over 45 where sample sizes were very small.[7] No study shows that those attending secondary school marry younger than primary graduates.

Some studies indicate the relation between post-secondary education and age of marriage, but such information seems to be irrelevant for population policy considerations in developing countries. By far

7. These differences are not uniform at all age groups, since the youngest age groups exclude women who have yet to marry, that is, have ages of marriages far above the mean for each group.

the largest differences and the most uniform effect is that of secondary education. This results, no doubt, from the fact that secondary education directly conflicts with marriage and, in itself, is an alternative to early marriage which is independent of job markets. However, the fact that in all cases those completing secondary school have an average age of marriage in excess of 20, and generally over 21, indicates that the impact of secondary school goes far beyond the simple act of keeping adolescent girls off the street or, rather, out of the marriage market and in the classroom.

In two of the three studies that report on urban and rural data separately, there is some evidence that the relation of education to age of marriage differs somewhat by residence. Among those who have been married 1 to 4 years in the Kerala India study (but not among those married 10 to 14 years), the difference in age of marriage between those with elementary and those with high school is much larger in rural than in urban areas. In Turkey (Stycos and Weller, 1967) the educated always marry later than the uneducated, but among working women the difference in urban areas is more than twice the difference in rural areas. Among unemployed women the differences by educational status are nearly identical in urban and rural areas. In the Lapierre-Adamcyk and Burch studies of Korea there appear to be very few differences in urban and rural areas in the relation between education and age of marriage. Smith (1977) also approached the issue of the interaction of education and urban residence in the analysis of age of marriage in Asia without finding a clear pattern of interaction.

In addition to these urban-rural differences in actual age of marriage by educational group, Paydarfar (1975) has reported on the ideal age of marriage that Iranian men reported for their sons and daughters. In urban areas these ideals for daughters were significantly positively related to the father's (and his wife's) education. Among rural and tribal groups no significant relation was reported. In none of the groups was the ideal age for sons significantly related to education.[8]

MULTIPLE REGRESSION PATTERNS. The most sophisticated studies methodologically are those few multiple regression studies of the age

---

8. The lack of significance in rural and tribal areas may result from the smaller sample sizes in that area. It would have been helpful if Paydarfar had reported the value of correlations coefficients as well as the significance.

of marriage. Kogut's study of Brazil (1974), Knowles and Anker's study of Kenya (1975), and Harmon's study of the Philippines (1970) provide straightforward confirmation of the effect of the wife's education on the age of marriage. In each case the coefficient is positive and significant.[9] Kogut also found that the male's education had a positive significant coefficient for equations of the male's age at marriage, but in each instance the wife's education had a greater effect.

The magnitude of the effect of education on the age of marriage differs by region and age group. In Brazil, the coefficient was 0.3 or larger, indicating that, at the average level of education, an increase of 1 year of schooling would increase the age of marriage by about a third of a year. The only other coefficient of this magnitude was among 25- to 29-year-olds in the Philippines. In Kenya, the coefficient was only 0.08. Part of the difference in effect may reflect the different average level of education in each group. In Kenya, the average level of education was only 3.63, but in the Philippines it ranged from 3.24 for women over 44 for whom education had no significant effect to 6.44 among women 30 to 34 where the coefficient was 0.28. Average education of women is not given by region for the Brazilian data.

Although the CELADE study (1972) does not provide zero and multiple correlation analysis of age at first marriage, it does contain such analysis for ideal age of marriage.[10] The wife's education and that of her husband are positively correlated with the ideal age at first marriage in all nine cities. In multiple correlation, wife's education is significantly positively correlated in all cases except San Jose and Quito.[11] In multiple correlation, husband's education is only significantly correlated in one case, San Jose, and here it is positively correlated.

In summary, the bulk of evidence indicates that increases in female education increase the age of marriage, as hypothesized. The exceptions to this pattern tend to result from the fact that, in certain circumstances, those with no education at all tend to marry later than

9. The only exception is for women over 44 in the Philippine's study where the coefficient is not significant.

10. This is the age that women report as being ideal for first marriage. Yaukey and Thorsen show that "whereas there was a marked association between high education and later ideal marriage, there was at least marked association in that direction for real marriage."

11. Yaukey and Thorsen found that in San Jose the least-educated married later.

those with some primary education. In some instances, those with no education also had fewer children than those with a few years of schooling.

The effect of male education on age of marriage is much less clear because of the scarcity of data, but male age of marriage is less important than female age in determining the biological supply of children. Unfortunately, the studies relating education to age of marriage do not contain enough rural studies to determine if there are urban-rural differences in the effect of education on the age of marriage. However, the Stycos and Weller study of Turkey seems to indicate that employment, education, and residence may have important interaction effects on age of marriage which need to be studied further. The size of the effect of education seems to be greater at the secondary than at the primary school level, but there is also wide variation from country to country in these differences.

Education and Fecundity

The biological supply of births depends not only on the number of years of marriage and thus the age of marriage, but also on the fecundity of those years. It can be assumed that the more educated are in better health and are thus more fecund.[12] Unfortunately, it is difficult to acquire the kind of data necessary to test this hypothesis. A few pieces of information do exist, however. Several studies give insight into the ways in which education might be related to fecundity.

In the first study, Jain (1969) estimated fecundity by the length of time between marriage and first birth for 2,190 women who had not been premaritally pregnant and who had not used contraception during this interval. Multiple classification analysis showed that, after controlling for the wife's age at marriage, those of the highest education group (husband's or wife's education) had higher probabilities of conception than the least educated, but the relation was not always uniform for adjacent educational groups. However, it appears that fecundity depends more on the husband's education than on the

---

12. See Butz and Habicht (1976) and Baird (1965) for discussions of the link between health status and fecundity. The Butz-Habicht definition of fecundity as the capacity of a woman to have children is followed here. Fertility represents the actual number of children born rather than the capacity to bear them.

wife's, and, in fact, the husband's education is the strongest predictor of fecundity. Thus, another reason for the weaker negative effect of male education on completed fertility is its positive relation with fecundity probably acting through income.

Another study in Taiwan (Jain and others, 1970) deals with factors affecting fecundity after the birth of a child rather than fecundity before the first birth. This study examined the effect of education, residence, age, and number of births on lactation and postpartum amenorrhea. In this study, the authors found that "better education or urban residence goes with younger age and a shorter period of lactation and that these in turn shorten the period of amenorrhea. In this way modernization may act to increase the period of child-bearing risk." Yaukey (1963) found that, in urban areas, educated women nursed their children for a shorter time than the uneducated in Lebanon. Adegbola and others (1977) also found this to be true in two urban samples in Nigeria. In their preliminary work on Malaysia, Butz and DaVanzo (1978) found that when other variables were controlled in multiple regression, the mother's education was only significantly related to length of partial breast feeding for those who breastfed and not to probability of breast feeding, length of feeding, or length of full feeding. With respect to partial breast feeding, the effect of education was negative as expected. In the Malaysian World Fertility Survey (Chandler and Palan, 1977) both mean months of breast feeding and proportion feeding were inversely related to education of women and also to income of the husband. The Nepal World Fertility Survey (1977) shows that if either husband or wife had some schooling, the woman was less likely to breast feed for 2 years or more.

Other evidence is related to observance of postpartum abstinence. Hull and Hull (1977), using Indonesian data, related the length of voluntary postpartum abstinence to income level and found a fairly uniform pattern of shorter periods of abstinence among higher income groups of each age. Adegbola and others related such abstinence in urban Nigeria to education and found the higher the level of education, the shorter the duration of abstinence.

Thus, education appears to increase the potential supply of births through biological and behavioral factors—through health as measured by the probability of conception, through breast feeding practices, and through observance of postpartum abstinence. In all cases, the relations suggest higher natural fertility among the wealthier and the more educated.[13] Whether such results can be generalized to other populations is uncertain. Even if the fecundity in each year of marriage were unaffected by education, it is still likely that the supply of surviving children would be affected by education because of the relation of education to infant and child mortality.

Education and Infant and Child Mortality

The supply of surviving children depends not only on the supply of births but also on the proportion of these births that survive. It can be assumed that the children of the more educated have higher survival rates. There is also some empirical support for such a relation. In this section a number of cross-national, cross-regional, and cross-individual studies of this relation are discussed. Table 3.3 shows the results of these studies.

Cross-national patterns

Shin (1975) and Stockwell and Hutchinson (1975) have conducted cross-national studies of the relation between infant mortality rates and education. Stockwell and Hutchinson found that adult literacy was significantly negatively correlated with infant and post-neonatal mortality rates. In addition, the correlation coefficients were second in importance only to percent of calories from animal protein. However, when the sample was split on the basis of the dependent variable, literacy did not have a significant effect in countries with high infant mortality. In addition, in countries at lower levels of mortality only post-neonatal mortality was related significantly to literacy.[14]

Shin, using data for 1958 and 1968, found that newspaper circulation had significantly negative correlations with infant mortality for developing countries in both time periods. However, in multiple re-

13. Another way education may increase fertility is by reducing adult mortality, thus increasing the number of years of exposure to pregnancy. Data on this relation were not surveyed.

14. Post-neonatal mortality covers the period from 1 month to 1 year of age. Neonatal rates are calculated for deaths in the first month of life. Post-neonatal rates are more influenced by environmental factors and less by congenital factors than neonatal or total infant mortality rates.

Table 3.3. *Evidence on Education and Infant and Child Mortality*

Study (date published)	Location (sample size)	Method	Direction of relation
Cross-national			
Shin (1975)	1960 and 1970 censuses	correlation multiple regression	inverse[a] inverse[a]
Stockwell and Hutchinson (1975)	censuses late 1960s	correlation high mortality low mortality moderate mortality	inverse[a] inverse inverse[a] inverse[a]
Cross-regional			
Heller (1976)	Malaysia census—1947, 57, 70	multiple regression (1970) (1947, 57, 70 pooled)	(F) infant—inverse[a] toddler—inverse[a] (F) infant—inverse[a] toddler—mixed
Sloan (1971)	Costa Rica Mexico	multiple regression multiple regression	(F) infant—inverse[a] preschool—inverse[a] (F) infant—inverse[a] direct (1960) preschool—inverse
Sloan (1971)	East Pakistan	multiple regression	(F) infant—direct[a] preschool—inverse
Sloan (1971)	Puerto Rico	multiple regression	(F) infant—mixed
Cross-individual			
Butz and DaVanzo (1978)	1976–77 survey (4,067)	multiple regression	(F) inverse[a]
Cochrane and others (1977)	Nepal 1976 survey (144)	multiple regression	(M) mixed (not significant
Hull and Hull (1977)	Indonesia 1971 census	cross-tabular	(F) urban—inverse (F) rural—inverse
Kelley (1976)	Kenya urban survey (401)	multiple regression	(M) inverse[a]
Khalifa (1976)	Egypt 1973 survey (1,234)	cross-tabular	(F) rural—inverse[a]
Khan and Sirageldin (1975)	Pakistan 1968–69 survey (2,910)	multiple regression	(M) inverse (F) direct

Table 3.3   (continued)

Study (date published)	Location (sample size)	Method	Direction of relation
Knowles and Anker (1975)	Kenya survey (1,074)	multiple regression	(F) inverse[a]
Olusanya (1971)	Nigeria 1966 survey (4,408)	cross-tabular	(F) inverse—perceived mortality
Singh (1974)	India survey (311)	cross-tabular	(F) working—inverse nonworking—no relation
Stycos (1968)	Peru survey (1,995)	cross-tabular	(F) Lima—inverse (perceived mortality)

Note: (F) = education of women; (M) = education of men.
a. Statistically significant.
Sources: For complete references, see the sources for this chapter.

gression equations including measures of urbanization, population for each physician, and a measure of development, newspaper circulation was only marginally significant in developing countries but was highly significant in developed countries.

These two studies indicate that in the poorest of environments, there are perhaps fewer opportunities for parents to affect their children's health through the improved knowledge of, or the better access to, medical care associated with education. In addition, the Stockwell and Hutchinson study indicates that measures of mortality that are unrelated to the immediate circumstance of birth are more influenced by environmental factors and thus by variables such as parents' education. Sloan's cross-regional multiple regression studies in Costa Rica, Mexico, East Pakistan, and Puerto Rico (1971) and Heller's cross-regional study of West Malaysia (1976) shed light on these issues.

Cross-regional patterns

Of these countries, Puerto Rico has the lowest infant mortality rate for the periods studied. In the Puerto Rican results, few of the mortality differences can be explained by the various factors, and female literacy is not significant and in fact fluctuates in sign. Perhaps this indicates that in countries with very low mortality, parents' education has little effect, at least when aggregates are being analyzed.

The infant mortality rate in Puerto Rico was 42.1 for every 1,000 births, but East Pakistan, with a rate of 171.4, had the highest rate of the four countries. Again, in this high infant mortality country, female literacy was not statistically significant, and its coefficient was positive rather than negative.

The results for the countries with middle mortality levels—Mexico and Costa Rica—are in striking contrast to the countries with high and low mortality. In Costa Rica, with an infant mortality rate of 53.9, female literacy had a significantly negative regression coefficient in equations for both infant mortality and preschool mortality. Mexico, with higher infant mortality rates than Costa Rica (90 in 1950 and 70 in 1960), showed no significant relation between infant mortality and female literacy but did show significantly negative regression coefficients in the preschool mortality equation. In addition, in both Costa Rica and Mexico preschool mortality was much better explained by literacy and other environmental variables than was infant mortality.

Heller's cross-regional study of West Malaysia gives varying results depending on the period studied.[15] For 1970, when the infant death rates was fairly low at 39 for every 1,000, female literacy had a significantly negative regression coefficient for infant but not toddler mortality. In the cross-regional data pooled for 1947, 1957, and 1970, the total female literacy rate is significantly negative for infant mortality. However in the toddler mortality equations, the percentages of Chinese and Indian women who were literate tended to have significantly positive coefficients although the percentage of literate Malay women had significantly negative coefficients. These results are somewhat difficult to interpret, however, since they combine ethnicity and education. From these results infant mortality appears to be inversely related to female education in both data sets, but toddler mortality is less well behaved. This tends to contradict Sloan's findings that pre-school mortality is more explainable.

---

15. Heller's regression model is quite different from Sloan's since fertility and mortality are entered as endogenous variables in Heller's study, that is, mortality and fertility are assumed to be determined simultaneously rather than for one to determine the other.

Cross-individual patterns

As mentioned in earlier parts of this study, aggregate relations need not hold at the individual level, and it is the relation between parent's education and child mortality that is relevant for this model. Thus the existing evidence on the individual relation is also presented in Table 3.3.

The cross-tabular evidence is rather sparse. The Indonesian data (Hull and Hull, 1977) are the best and show inverse relations between education and infant mortality in urban and rural areas. The study of rural Egypt (Khalifa, 1976) and the small Indian study (Singh, 1974) also show inverse relations except for the nonworking women in the Indian study. In Indonesia, rural Egypt, and for the working women in India, the mortality of offspring for the most educated women is less than half that of the least educated. The Nigerian (Olusanya, 1971) and Peruvian (Stycos, 1968) studies also show that the more educated are more likely to perceive that mortality has been falling over time.

The multiple regression results are mixed. The two Kenya studies (Knowles and Anker, 1975; Kelley, 1976) show inverse relations that are statistically significant—in one case for male and in one case for female education. The Pakistan study (Khan and Sirageldin, 1975) enters both the husband's and the wife's education in the same equation. None of these variables have significant coefficients, but three of the four are inverse. In each case, income was inversely related to child mortality, and in one case it was significant. Income was not significant in either study of Kenya, although its coefficient showed an inverse association in all cases. In the small-scale Nepalese pretest (Cochrane, 1977) the six measures of male education and educational outcomes (literacy, numeracy, and so forth) fluctuated in sign. Only years of school completed, which was inverse, approached significance. In all cases income was inversely related to child mortality, but in no case was it significant. The Butz-DaVanzo study of Malaysia (1978) showed that female education was inversely related to infant mortality, but this was only significant if measures of housing quality were not included in the equation. Thus, it appears the association of education with higher income and better living conditions is responsible for the association with lower infant and child mortality, but this is not a universal pattern.

Summary

The biological supply of children depends on the years of exposure to pregnancy, which is determined by the age of marriage, the potential fertility (fecundity) of those years, and the survival of offspring. There is good reason to believe that education affects all these factors through its effect on a wide range of opportunities. Education provides men and women with more choices about their lives. This affects their decisions to marry and at what age.

Education also increases the possibilities for improved health for parent and child by providing better knowledge and higher income. The effect of education on the decision to marry is less predictable than its effect on health because circumstances and values about the desirability of marriage differ widely, but improved health is generally highly valued. Education is not universally associated with improved health, probably because certain environments are either so healthy or so unhealthy that individuals at all educational levels can either have good access to health care or no access whatsoever and are fully exposed to the same environmental circumstances.

The effect of education on marriage varies widely depending on the kind of society and on the sex of the individual. In the developed countries of the West, the effect of literacy seems fairly unimportant. In the less developed countries, female education has a fairly strong direct relation with age of marriage, but there is some evidence that this effect may be second to, and probably acts through, female labor participation prior to marriage. For males, the effect of education on age of marriage is less uniform and less strong. Female education in developing countries is usually inversely related to the proportion of women who marry before the end of the childbearing period. The effect on the proportion of males ever marrying is unclear. Thus, education tends to decrease fertility by reducing the exposure to pregnancy for women through increasing the age of marriage and reducing the proportion married.

However, education increases the potential number of surviving children for each year of marriage. What little evidence exists indicates that fecundity, as measured by the potential supply of births in each year of marriage, is greater because of better health, less rigid observance of sexual postpartum taboos, and shorter lactation periods.

The survival of infants is also more probable for the more educated, but this effect is not equally strong everywhere and seems to be strongest at middle levels of mortality.[16]

Thus education has positive and negative effects on the unregulated supply of children; it seems to lower the years spent in marriage but raises the biological supply of living children for each year of marriage. The effects of education on the demand for children are expected to be more generally negative.

16. The biological effect of improved survival is to increase the number of surviving children. However, such an effect may generate behavioral adjustments to reduce the number of children ever born by acting through the demand for an additional child and fertility regulation.

4

Education and the Demand
for Children

In the previous chapter, the relations between education
and several factors determining the biological supply of children—
age of marriage, fecundity, infant mortality, and practices of lactation
and postpartum abstinence—were examined. In this section the relations between education and factors determining the demand for
children—perceived costs and benefits of children and ideal family
size—are discussed.

Factors Determining the Demand for Children

The demand for an additional child depends directly on the desired family size (demand for children) and the current family size.
The latter depends on previous fertility and on infant and child
mortality. Since it was shown in the previous chapter that education
is generally inversely related to such mortality, it is expected that
education, through this variable, also reduces the demand for an
additional birth and therefore the total demand for births. Its effect

on the demand for surviving children is less certain since reduced mortality lowers the "price" of surviving children. Since the evidence strongly supports a positive relation between infant and child mortality and births, it seems apparent that reduced mortality increases the demand for surviving children less than it increases the biological supply of surviving children. The factors that determine desired family size (other than mortality) for which adequate data exist are discussed below.

In terms of the model developed in Figure 2.2, desired family size (the substitute for the static demand for children) depends on preferences and perceptions of the various costs and benefits of children as well as on the ability to afford children. The data on these variables are relatively scarce, in part because the precise meaning of the terms used in the theoretical model are not clarified.

This seems to be a major problem with the concept of income. Current income is often used rather than some lifetime measure of potential income. Part of the ambiguity in the relation between income and fertility results from the use of improper measures of income. Thus, although it might be interesting to determine the relation between husband's education and income in developing countries, this information tells little about the fertility-education relation since the income-fertility link is not known.[1] Thus, no attempt will be made to inventory the evidence on the education-income link.

The ability to afford children depends on income and the "price" of children. No such price is, of course, observable, although theoretical models of shadow prices have been developed. Rather than trying to specify a concept of price, it is easier to use the concept of the costs of children.[2] The economist is interested in separating these costs into money cost and time cost, because such a distinction is vital to understanding the interaction of female education, market

1. Chapter 1 provides some data on this relation. In the thirty-one regression equations reported, income was significant in one-third of the cases. Half of the significant coefficients were negative, and half were positive.

2. The price-cost issue is quite complex, since many of the expenditures made on children are not required by the market. The market dictates the price of rice, but the cost of feeding a child depends on how much of what items it is fed. These discretionary expenditures have been labeled child quality by Becker (1960). Required expenditures will not be separated from discretionary expenditures in this discussion.

work, and fertility. Unfortunately, too little data have been collected in developing countries to allow the time costs of children and their relation to female education to be estimated.[3] There is more evidence on the monetary costs, since several studies have been conducted on the perceived monetary costs of children of people of various characteristics. There is also data from the same studies on the perceived benefits of children in terms of child labor and old age security.

The relation between level of education and preferences for children can best be estimated by examining data on ideal family size. Although ideal family size is not a measure of relative preferences, it does give some insight into family size preferences unconstrained by economic considerations.

Therefore, the effect of education on the demand for children will first be examined by looking at the relation between education and family size preferences and between education and the perceived costs and benefits of children. The net effect of education, through these variables, on the demand for children can be evaluated by looking at the relation between education and a measure of the constrained preferences for children, desired family size.[4]

Preferences for Children (Ideal Family Size)

A number of studies of ideal family size are summarized in Table 4.1. Urban Latin America is well represented by the CELADE studies. Asia is represented by studies of Taiwan, Korea, Thailand, and India. Continental Africa is represented by three studies of Nigeria and one each for Sierra Leone and Egypt. Most of the evidence shows inverse relations between education and ideal family size. In Latin America,

3. Exceptions are the study of Thailand by Maurer and others (1973) and Rosenzweig's study of rural India (1976), which use areal aggregate data and estimate the relation between female education and the wages of women. In Thailand female education had the expected effect. In the Indian study, the percentage of women with primary schooling did not have a significant coefficient in the equation for the female wage rate.

4. This distinction between the ideal or unconstrained and desired or constrained preferences may seem somewhat artificial, but evidence shows that there are systematic differences in responses to questions about ideal family size in general and questions about the ideal family size for a person in the circumstances of the respondent. See Freedman, R., Goldberg, D., and Sharp, H. (1955), and Ware (1974) for discussions of these issues.

however, Buenos Aires and Rio de Janeiro fail to show inverse correlations for female education (CELADE, 1972). In fact Buenos Aires shows significant positive partial correlations between education and ideal family size when other variables are controlled. Korea shows a very slight upturn in ideal family size among women who have gone beyond high school (Chung, 1972). Males in Taichung City, Taiwan (Freedman and others, 1962), and females under 45 in Cairo (Khalifa, 1973) showed irregular association between education and ideal family size. Slight direct relations were found in two groups in the India study, but these were not significant (Pareek and Kothandapani, 1969). The India study showed that the inverse relation between education and ideal fertility was much more likely to be significant for urban and rural industrial workers than for cultivators or nonindustrial urban workers.

Differences in ideal family size by educational groups

Some of the cross-tabular studies also give evidence about the size of the differences in ideal family size by educational group. Differences in ideal family sizes between the most educated and the least educated in these cross-tabular comparisons range from 0.03 to 1.75 children. The smallest difference is for young women in Cairo (Khalifa, 1973). The largest difference is observed in Korea (Chung, 1972). In Taiwan, the educational differences slightly increased between 1965 and 1973 despite overall drops in ideal family sizes for all groups (Freedman and others, 1974). In Thailand, the educational differences in urban areas were almost twice those in rural areas, perhaps explaining why differences in completed family size are smaller in rural areas (Knodel and Pitakepsombati, 1973). In Sierra Leone, the differences in ideal family size by education were largest in the capital of Freetown, followed by the differences in towns (Dow, 1971). In the villages the differences were less than half as large as those in Freetown.[5]

---

5. The differences in ideal family size by educational level may over- or underestimate the true impact on family size preferences. Two women may state ideal family sizes of two, but if given a second choice one might say one and the other three, and on third choice one may say zero and the other four. These two women would have very different preferences for children despite identical ideal (first choice) family size preferences. Lolagene Coombs (1975) has developed a technique for estimating these underlying preferences.

Table 4.1. *Evidence on Education and Family Size Preferences (Ideal Family Size)*

Study (date published)	Location (sample size)	Method	Direction of relation
CELADE (1972)	9 Latin American cities	Zero-order correlations (see Table 1.5)	(F) inverse except Buenos Aires and Rio de Janeiro
		Partial correlation	(F) inverse[a] in Mexico City, Quito, and Guayaquil; direct[a] in Buenos Aires
Chung (1972)	Korea (1,883)	cross-tabular	(F) inverse through senior high school then slight upturn
Dow (1971)	Sierra Leone (5,952)	cross-tabular	(F) literary inverse, schooling inverse
Freedman and others (1963)	Taichung City, Taiwan (1962) (241 couples)	cross-tabular	(M) curvilinear
Freedman and others (1974)	Taiwan (1965–73) (14,920)	cross-tabular	(F) inverse
Khalifa (1973)	Cairo, Egypt (569)	cross-tabular	(F) over 45—inverse (F) under 45— curvilinear (M) inverse
Knodel and Pitakepsombati (1973)	Thailand (2,000 urban; 1,500 rural)	cross-tabular	(F) urban—inverse (F) rural—inverse

Additional differences are found in Sierra Leone. Dow showed fertility differences both by literacy and by whether the women had ever attended school. For the country as a whole and for the capital and various towns and villages, the differences for literacy were somewhat smaller than for school attendance, indicating that the act of attending school may affect family size preferences beyond providing literacy itself.

Perhaps one of the most interesting results was that found by Olusanya in western Nigeria (1971). The proportion of women who felt that fertility was "up to God" decreased from over 50 percent for those with no schooling to under 10 percent for those who went beyond primary school. This is perhaps one of the most important

Table 4.1   (*continued*)

Study (date published)	Location (sample size)	Method	Direction of relation
Ohadike (1969)	Lagos, Nigeria (596)	Zero-order correlation	(F) inverse (M) inverse
Olusanya (1971)	western Nigeria (4,408)	cross-tabular	(F) inverse
Pareek and Kothandapani (1969)	India (1,500)	cross-tabular	(M) significantly inverse—generally for urban and rural factory workers (M) Generally not significantly inverse for cultivators and nonindustrial urban work
Ware (1975)	western Nigeria (1,495 men; 1,495 women)	cross-tabular	(M) inverse (F) inverse
Yaukey (1963)	Lebanon (613)	cross-tabular	(F) inverse but differences are minute

Note: (M) = education of men; (F) = education of women.
a. Statistically significant.
Sources: For complete references, see the sources for this chapter.

effects of education. Those who feel fertility is solely up to God end up with family sizes determined by supply factors. Only when this position is abandoned can demand factors operate, which may lead to fertility limitation. Yaukey (1963) found that in urban Lebanon more educated women were more likely to express explicit opinions about ideal family size than were uneducated women. However, the differences in ideal family size of those who expressed opinions by education were too small to be significant.

Preference for sons

In the entire discussion so far the issue of preference for sons has been ignored. The more sons desired, the greater the family size needed to obtain the ideal number of sons. Thus, if preference for sons decreases with increased education, the desired family size will

Table 4.2. *Mean Ideal Number of Sons for Married Women 20 to 39 Years Old, by Wife's Education and Urban-Rural Residence*

| | Mean ideal number of sons | | | | | | | | | | | |
Item	Calcutta 1970	Delhi 1968–69	India 1970	Rural East Java 1972	Korea 1971	West Malaysia 1966–67	West Malaysia 1970	Philippines 1968	Taiwan 1967	Belgium 1966	Hungary 1966	United States 1970
Wife's education												
No formal	2.1	1.9	2.3	2.1	2.5	2.6	2.5	3.5	2.2	—b	2.4	—a
Primary	1.9	1.8	2.2	1.9	2.2	2.5	2.3	2.8	2.1	1.1	1.1	—a
Junior high	1.7	1.7	—a	1.6	2.0	2.3	2.0	2.6	1.9	1.2	0.9	1.7
Senior high and over	1.4	1.5	1.9	2.2	1.8	2.0	1.9	2.4	1.8	1.3	0.9	1.4
Urban-rural residence												
Large city	—a	—a	2.0	—a	2.0	2.2	2.1	2.5	2.0	1.1	0.8	1.5
Small city	—a	—a	2.0	—a	2.2	2.4	2.3	2.4	2.1	1.2	1.0	1.5
Urban township	—a	—a	2.1	—a	2.1	—a	—a	2.9	2.2	1.2	1.0	1.5
Rural township	—a	—a	2.3	—a	2.4	2.7	2.4	2.8	2.2	1.3	1.1	1.6
Total	1.8	1.8	2.2	2.0	2.2	2.5	2.4	2.7	2.1	1.2	1.0	1.5
Sample size	947	5,242	10,246	411	1,620	4,242	11,918	28,632c	4,300	2,566	5,208	4,685

Note: See Appendix 1, items 1, 6, and 8 of source for definitions.
a. Less than 20 cases in the category.
b. No such category.
c. Frequency weighted as follows: urban respondents × 4 and rural respondents × 12.
Source: R. Freedman and L. Coombs, *Cross-Cultural Comparisons: Data on Two Factors in Fertility Behavior* (New York: The Population Council, 1974).

also decrease, all other things being equal. Freedman and Coombs (1974) have reported on ideal number of sons by the wife's education in several Asian societies as well as for three developed countries. Their results are shown in Table 4.2. The only exceptions to an inverse relation between education and ideal number of sons occurs in rural East Java and Belgium. In developing countries the differences across education classes range from 0.4 in Taiwan and India to 1.1 in the Philippines. These differences partially reflect changes in overall family size that occur with increases in education but also reflect reductions in the proportion of sons desired.

Perceived Costs and Benefits of Children

Many of the explanations of the decline in fertility that accompanies economic development center on discussions of the changing costs and benefits of children brought about by the development process (Leibenstein, 1957). A number of studies on the value of children have attempted to document the relation between certain variables and these perceptions. Most of these studies have been conducted in Asian countries, and these results may not apply elsewhere. Studies relating these perceptions to the level of education are examined here.

The value of children study

This ambitious cross-national survey of the costs and benefits of children has been carried out at the East-West Center of the University of Hawaii. Table 4.3 reproduces the zero-order correlations between the individual's education and perceptions of five aspects of the economic costs and benefits of children (Arnold, 1975). The most consistent pattern associated with these variables is the inverse relation between the parents' education and their expectations of economic help from their children. Although the size of the correlations varied in relation to this benefit of children, they were all significant at the 1 percent level.

The relation between education of parents and their concern for the economic burden of educating children is inverse in all cases and significant in every case except Japan. This does not mean that the more educated spend less on their children's education, but rather

Table 4.3. *Zero-Order Correlations between Education and Perceived Costs and Benefits of Children*

Cost or benefit	Country				
	Korea	Taiwan	Japan	Philippines	Thailand
Economic burden of education	−0.44[a]	−0.42[a]	−0.05	−0.32[a]	−0.36[a]
Financial ease of large family[c]	0.02	0.16[a]	0.15[a]	−0.02	−0.04
Expected economic help from children	−0.65[a]	−0.59[a]	−0.22[a]	−0.34[a]	−0.71[a]
Decreased utility of children	0.08[b]	0.20[a]	−0.06	0.26[a]	0.16[a]
Economic benefits of large families	−0.07	−0.17[a]	0.10	−0.22[a]	−0.17[a]
Sample size	378	432	412	389	360

a. Statistically significant at the 1 percent level.
b. Statistically significant at the 5 percent level.
c. Ability to afford a large family.
Source: Fred Arnold, and others, *The Value of Children: A Cross-National Study*, Volume I (Honolulu: The East-West Center, 1975), table 5.5.

that they feel such expenditures to be less of a burden than do the less educated. In Taiwan and Japan the more educated feel less financial difficulty in raising a large family than the less educated. In Korea, Philippines, and Thailand the correlations between education and the ability to afford children are not significantly different from zero.

In all countries except Japan, the more educated generally perceive that the utility of children has been declining[6] to a greater extent than do the less educated. In addition, in all countries except Korea and Japan the more educated are less likely to perceive economic benefits from large families. Thus on the three measures of the utility of and economic benefits from children, the more educated perceive less return from children than do the less educated. However, the more

6. This was measured by the perception that the current generation is less willing than the previous one to have parents live with them, to give part of wages to parents in old age, and to help in the house, farm, or business.

educated in these studies also appear to feel better able to afford children, which may offset some of the estimated effect of education on the perceived benefits of children. The World Fertility Survey in Thailand also found that the more educated expect less economic benefits from children and also showed that the most educated felt better able to afford children than the least educated. Those with a small amount of education felt the greatest economic burden from having four or fewer children (WFS, 1977).

The net effect of these positive and negative effects of education on the demand for children cannot be determined from this study. However, Bulatao (1975) has used the Philippines data to construct regressions of ideal family size on several demographic variables and measures of costs and benefits. For urban and rural samples, marital duration was significantly positively related to ideal family size. In all samples, the number of children perceived as imposing a heavy financial burden was significantly positively related to ideals. In rural areas, the help expected from children had a positive relation with ideal family size. In urban areas those who felt there were benefits to large families had significantly larger ideal family sizes. In those regressions, education itself failed to be significantly related to ideals when other demographic variables and values were controlled. Thus education appears to act through these perceived costs and benefits in determining ideal family size.

Other studies on the costs and benefits of children

The simplest of such studies are those like Olusanya's (1971) which ask whether more children tend to raise or lower the family's standard of living. In Western Nigeria, Olusanya found that the more educated were less likely to believe that having more children raised the standard of living.

Another interesting study on perceived costs of children is that reported by Eva Mueller (1972). This work was based on a 1969 survey of over 2,000 husbands in Taiwan conducted by the Population Studies Center of the University of Michigan. Mueller found that the perceived utility of children declined with education and with income. Husband's education, income for each adult, and wife's education rank first, second, and third, respectively, in importance in explaining the husband's perception of the utility of children. The husband's education and number of living children were the most important in explaining the husband's sensitivity to the cost of children.

Mueller also constructed a series of regression equations and measured the relative importance of cost sensitivity, perceived utility, income for each adult, and age of wife in explaining desired family size.[7] The results differed substantially depending on whether the wife was under or over 30 years old. For husbands with wives under 30, cost sensitivity, perceived utility, and husband's education were first, second, and third, respectively, in explaining desired family size. Thus husband's education has an impact above and beyond its effect on attitudes. For wives over 30, wife's education, cost sensitivity, age of wife, and perceived utility ranked in that order in explaining desired family size. One problem, of course, is that older couples are more likely to rationalize their own behavior by reporting desires quite close to actual family size. Thus education and age of the wife may have their effect through actual fertility.

In a later paper, Mueller and Cohn (1977) used path analysis to determine how several variables affect desired family size through the intervening variables of educational aspirations for children, perceived benefits of children, and consumption aspirations. Although education's effect through these variables is not discussed explicitly, it can be deduced by using the path coefficients given in figure 2 of the study. The correlation of wife's education and desired family size is —0.26, which in absolute size exceeds correlation of desired family size with income. This correlation can be broken down to direct, indirect, and interaction effects. The direct effect is somewhat over half the total (—0.14). Of the indirect effects, the effect of education through the perceived benefits of children is the largest, followed by its effect through consumer aspirations, and then by the effect through the father's aspirations for his child's education. The failure of education to have a stronger impact on fertility through educational aspirations for children is unexpected and may be peculiar to Taiwan.

Another study on the benefits of children in Asia was conducted

---

7. Mueller refers to this as ideal family size, but in a later article the question used to elicit the information appears to be more closely related to desired family size, since it implicitly incorporated an income constraint. The actual question was, "If you were just getting married and could have just the number of children you want, how many would you like to have had when your wife is through having children, about age 45?"

by Chang in Singapore (1976). Subjective measures of the benefits and the costs of children and the ability to afford children were obtained for 900 Chinese women who had their first, second, or third child in the spring of 1972. These measures of the benefits and costs were related to seven demographic and economic variables. The wife's education was the most important of these variables in explaining both benefits and costs. The type of education was the second most important variable explaining the benefits of children. Those women trained in English rather than Chinese schools had lower perceived utility for children. Wife's employment and husband's income were also usually important particularly after the second and third child, but husband's education was the least important explanatory variable. The direction of these variables was as expected: employed women had lower evaluations of children than other women, and higher husband's income was related to lower perceived benefits of children.

For the costs of children, wife's education is followed by employment and type of education (in different orders) for the second and third children and for the sample as a whole, but for women with their first child, husband's education is second in importance. The husband's income ranges from fourth to seventh in importance. As a whole, the demographic and economic variables explain the benefits of children better than they explain the costs.

Despite the importance of the wife's education in determining the subjective evaluation of the benefits and costs of children, the wife's education is unimportant in explaining the perceived ability to afford children. In fact, this ability is very poorly explained by the variables included, and ranking of variables by importance shifts greatly depending on which child is considered. Thus, while the perceived costs and benefits of children depend greatly on the wife's education and employment in this sample, the perceived ability to afford children does not.

When the three subjective variables were used to predict desired family size, ability to afford children was more important by far than costs or benefits of children for all children. If household income is used rather than the perceived ability to afford children, benefits and costs become more important in explaining desired family size, particularly after the first child. However, the use of actual income rather than the perceived ability to afford children substantially reduces the overall explanatory power of the model. Thus, the effect of education on desired fertility in this study must be assessed through its effect on the perceived costs of, benefits of, and ability to afford children.

Desired Family Size

As mentioned at the beginning of this chapter, preferences and perceived costs and benefits are considered to be factors that determine desired family size. The net impact of these various channels through which education acts can be estimated by examining the relation between education and desired fertility. There is unfortunately a degree of bias in questions of desired family size. Since this question is usually asked of women who have already borne children, desired fertility may represent some rationalization of actual fertility, and those who have little ability to control fertility may have to do more rationalizing. Thus educational differences may be exaggerated. This was a less serious problem when ideal fertility was examined, since ideals are not as specific to the individual's situation.

The studies of desired family size summarized in Table 4.4 are fairly limited in number. In Latin America, zero-order correlations between education and desired fertility are negative for women except in Buenos Aires and Bogotá (CELADE, 1972). Partial correlations show female education has significantly negative coefficients in only two cities and a significantly positive coefficient in Buenos Aires.[8]

In an early, small study of Taiwan by Freedman and others (1963), the relation between education and desired fertility for males and females was generally inverse, but somewhat irregular. The more recent survey of females by Speare and others (1973) found a regular inverse relation for urban and rural women with and without work experience. In addition, multiple classification analysis showed education to be the most important variable in explaining desired fertility. While Speare and others did not control for actual number of children, an age control was used.

The Ghanaian survey (Pool, 1970) shows inverse relations for both urban and rural regions. The West Malaysian survey (Palmore and

8. As hypothesized in the previous paragraph, desired family size is closely related to current family size in the CELADE data. This correlation is positive and significant after controlling for other variables in every country.

Table 4.4. *Evidence on Education and Desired Family Size*

Study (date published)	Location (sample size)	Method	Direction of relation
CELADE (1972)	9 Latin American cities	zero-order correlations (see Table 1.5)	(F) inverse except Buenos Aires, Rio, and Bogotá
		Partial correlation	(F) inverse[a] for Mexico City and Guayaquil; direct[a] for Buenos Aires
Freedman and others (1963)	Taichung City (241 couples)	cross-tabular	(M) inverse but irregular (F) inverse but irregular
Palmore and others (1969)	West Malaysia (5,457)	cross-tabular	(F) metropolitan— inverse nonmetropolitan urban—nonlinear rural—no difference
Paydarfar (1975)	Iran (1,062 urban) (176 rural) (146 tribal)	cross-tabular	(M) urban—inverse[a] rural and tribal— not significant
Pool (1970)	Ghana (5,700)	cross-tabular	(F) urban—inverse rural—inverse
Rizk (1977)	Jordan (1972) (5,214)	cross-tabular	(F) inverse through secondary school
Speare and others (1973)	Taiwan (3,579)	cross-tabular	(F) work experience away from home, urban and rural— inverse no work experience away, urban and rural—inverse
Weekes-Vagliani (1976)	Cameroon (213)	cross-tabular	(F) inverse[a]
World Fertility Survey (1977)	Nepal (5,665)	cross-tabular	(F) inverse
World Fertility Survey (1977)	Thailand (3,000)	cross-tabular	(F) inverse

Note: (M) = education of men; (F) = education of women.
a. Statistically significant.
Sources: For complete references, see the sources for this chapter.

Ariffin, 1969), however, shows strictly inverse relations only in urban metropolitan areas; rural areas show no differences by education level, and nonmetropolitan urban areas show higher desired fertility for those with some schooling than for those with no schooling. The authors also found that completed fertility was higher for women with some primary education than for women with more or less education.

The study of Iran (Paydarfar, 1975) shows desired family size that is negatively correlated with education at a significant level for urban males, but not for rural or tribal males. One problem with these results, however, is the small sample sizes in the rural and tribal areas. In the Rizk study of Jordan (1977), current family size was added to the additional number of children desired to get a substitute for total desired family size. An inverse relation was found through secondary school. The difference between illiterates and those with secondary schooling was more than four children.

The Weekes-Vagliani sample in Cameroon (1976) shows an inverse relation between education and desired family size in an urban and rural sample. While a test of independence showed a significant relation between education and desired fertility for the total sample, the sample size was too small to control for urban-rural residence as well as education. The Nepali (1976) and Thai (1977) World Fertility Surveys also show inverse relations. Thus the overall inverse relation is observed between education and desired family size, but the relation is not as consistent as that for ideal family size.

Summary

Education affects the demand for children by altering preferences and by changing the perceived costs, benefits, and ability to afford children. In Latin America, Buenos Aires and Rio de Janeiro tend to exhibit atypical effects.

Although education appears to be inversely related to ideal family size, a few nonlinear relations were observed, and the strength of the effect of education varies. The inverse relation with respect to the ideal number of sons is verified in all the developing countries except one. There are not enough cases, however, to determine if there are significant urban-rural, male-female, or literacy level differences in the relation.

The effect of education on perceived benefits was more uniform than that on preferences. Education was associated with a higher perceived ability to afford children but also with fewer perceived benefits from, and higher perceived costs of, children. The net effect of these factors generates an inverse relation between education and desired family size that tends to reduce the demand for children. Exceptions to this pattern occurred in Buenos Aires and nonmetropolitan West Malaysia.

Despite the evidence cited above, the linkages between education and the demand factors are not well established, and several crucial linkages are missing. The relation between female education, potential wages, and type of work available seem to be vital for testing the hypotheses set forward in the new home economics theory of fertility.[9] The effect of aggregate levels of female education on the cost of child care substitutes for the mother's time needs to be established if the interaction of individual and aggregate levels of education are to be understood. The effect of husband's income on the demand for children has been investigated frequently without conclusive results. This relation needs to be determined before the effect of husband's education on fertility can be established firmly.

9. The new home economics theory of fertility has grown out of Becker's original article on the economics of fertility. The theory attempts to examine the household's production of various goods—such as and including children—in a framework similar to that of the business firm. The various inputs to production are the time of various household members, particularly the wife, and goods purchased in the market. See Becker (1960) and Robert J. Willis (1973).

5

•-

Education and the Regulation of Fertility

The biological supply of children and the demand for children determine whether there is a potential demand for fertility regulation. However, the actual, and particularly the effective, use of contraception depends on several other factors. Attitudes toward fertility regulation, knowledge of birth control methods, access to the means of fertility regulation, and communication between husband and wife about family size goals are essential for effective fertility regulation. Where spouses have different desired family sizes, the balance of power between husband and wife[1] is also important in determining fertility regulation, but since the concepts of power are controversial and since power is not necessarily independent of the means of regulating fertility, the role of power will not be discussed in this review. The concept of access to the means of fertility regulation is also problematic because it depends on laws about provision

---

1. Economists might prefer to think of power in terms of the relative weights of each spouse's preferences in the family preference functions.

of birth control, income, and the availability of subsidized family planning services. Therefore, attitudes toward birth control, knowledge of contraception, and husband-wife communication are discussed in that order. The net effect of education through these variables can then be assessed by looking at the relation between education and contraception use. At a later stage, access is incorporated into the discussion.

Attitudes toward Birth Control

Table 5.1 summarizes a number of studies showing the relation between education and favorable attitudes toward birth control. Except for evidence of irregularities in Knodel and Pitakepsombati's study of Thailand (1973) and Palmore's study of West Malaysia (1969), the relation is always direct, but it does vary in significance and strength. The uniformity of the results in Table 5.1 is in striking contrast with the lack of uniformity in the relation between education and completed fertility reviewed earlier. Particularly in Latin America (CELADE, 1972) where a number of anomalous relations have been observed, there is no deviation from a direct relation between education and favorable attitudes toward birth control.[2] The study of India (Morrison, 1961) shows that education has some interaction with type of work. If a man is employed in factory work, education has less of an effect on attitude than otherwise, since most men in that environment have favorable attitudes regardless of their education.

Knowledge of Contraception and Education

Of course, a favorable attitude toward birth control is only the first step in successful practice. Knowledge of birth control methods is also essential.[3] Table 5.2 summarizes several studies relating contra-

---

2. Buenos Aires exhibited atypical results not only for completed family size but also for ideal family size.

3. This does not imply that knowledge follows attitude in any causal sense. Some minimal knowledge may be necessary to favorable attitudes. Some psychologists even feel that attitude follows use, that is, people validate their use of contraception by having favorable attitudes.

Table 5.1. *Evidence on Education and Attitudes*
toward Fertility Regulation

Study (date published)	Location (sample size)	Method	Direction of relation
CELADE (1972)	9 Latin American cities (1964–65)	zero-order correlations partial correlation (see Table 1.5)	(F) direct (H) direct (F) direct[a] in Mexico City (H) direct[a] in Mexico City
Dow (1971)	Sierra Leone (5,952)	cross-tabular	(F) literacy—direct (F) schooling—direct
Freedman and others (1963)	Taichung City, Taiwan (1962) (241 couples)	cross-tabular	(F) direct (M) direct
Khalifa (1976)	Egypt—rural (1,234)	cross-tabular	(F) direct
Knodel and Pitakepsombati (1973)	Thailand (1969–70) (3,500)	cross-tabular	(F) rural—direct, except 1 to 3 years approve less than no school urban—direct, except 4 years approve less than those with less schooling
Morgan (1975)	Nigeria (1964–68) (1,296)	cross-tabular	direct

ceptive knowledge and education. Again there is very strong support
for a direct relation. The major exception is again Thailand (Knodel
and Pitakepsombati, 1973), where those with 1 to 3 years of schooling
in rural areas are slightly less likely to know any method.[4] But even
in Thailand the general impact of education is as expected. This can
be seen from the fact that the education regression coefficient for
Thailand in the Value of Children Study (Arnold, 1975) is positive

4. The more recent 1976 World Fertility Survey in Thailand showed a uniformly direct relation between education and contraceptive knowledge. A very
rapid change in fertility and family planning knowledge and access occurred between 1969–70 and 1976.

Table 5.1   (*continued*)

Study (date published)	Location (sample size)	Method	Direction of relation
Morrison (1961)	India (1953) (290)	cross-tabular	(M) industrial— direct[a] village—direct[a]
Palmore (1969)	West Malaysia (5,457)	cross-tabular	(F) metropolitan— direct other urban— curvilinear rural—inverse
Pareek and Kothandapani (1969)	India (1,500)	cross-tabular	(M) cultivators and urban nonindustrial —direct urban and rural factory workers— direct
Pool (1970)	Ghana (1965–66) (5,700)	cross-tabular	direct
Williamson (1970)	India Israel Pakistan Chile Nigeria	zero-order correlation	direct direct direct direct direct

Note: (M) = education of men; (F) = education of women; (H) = husband's education of women.
   a. Statistically significant.
Sources: For complete references, see the sources for this chapter.

and significant. Likewise, although Palmore (1969) found atypical relations between education and attitudes toward contraception in nonmetropolitan West Malaysia, he found that the relation between education and knowledge of contraception was direct everywhere. In the study at Dacca by Roberts and others (1965) the only exception to a direct relation shows up in a group of women who have gone beyond the ninth grade. Since there are only nineteen women in the sample, this reversal in the general pattern is not significant.

The CELADE data (1972) indicates the relation between knowledge and education to be much stronger than that between attitude and education. The correlations for female education range from 0.331 to 0.47 for knowledge compared with 0.024 to 0.161 for attitude. The

Table 5.2. *Evidence on Education and Knowledge of Contraception*

Study (date published)	Location (sample size)	Method	Direction of relation
Arnold and others (1975)	Korea Taiwan Japan Philippines Thailand	Multiple regression (see Table 4.3)	(F) direct[a] (F) direct[a] (F) direct[a] (F) direct[a] (F) direct[a]
Caldwell and Igun (1975)	Nigeria (8,800)	cross-tabular	(F, M) direct
CELADE (1972)	9 Latin American cities (1964–65)	zero-order correlation partial correlation (see Table 1.5)	(F) direct (F) direct,[a] all cities
Chung and others (1972)	Korea (1971) (1,883)	cross-tabular	(F) direct[a]
Khalifa (1976)	Egypt—rural (1,234)	cross-tabular	(F) direct
Knodel and Pitakepsombati (1973)	Thailand (1969–70) (3,500)	cross-tabular	(F) urban—direct rural—direct except 1 to 3 years know less than less educated
Palmore (1969)	West Malaysia (5,457)	cross-tabular	(F) metropolian— direct other urban—direct rural—direct

Korean (Chung and others, 1972) and Thai cross-tabular studies indicate the magnitude of association. Of the Korean women who had no schooling, 78 percent had heard of at least one method. Of those who finished high school, 95 percent had heard of one. In Thailand the percent knowing a method ranged from 58.2 to 88.7 percent in urban areas, and in rural areas the range was 35.5 to 73.1. The difference in knowledge across educational classes in rural areas seemed greater than in urban areas. This pattern also appeared to be true in Morrison's comparison of industrial and village areas (1961). Caldwell and Igun (1975), however, found that while those with some schooling were more likely to know modern methods of contraception, the differences for urban areas were not necessarily smaller than in rural areas.

Table 5.2   (*continued*)

Study (date published)	Location (sample size)	Method	Direction of relation
Nepal Family Planning Survey	Nepal (1975) (6,012)	cross-tabular	(F) direct
Pool (1970)	Ghana (1965–66) (5,700)	cross-tabular	direct
Roberts and others (1965)	Dacca, East Pakistan (1962) (547M, 547F)	cross-tabular	(M) direct (F) direct through ninth grade
Simmons and de Jong	Rural Latin America Costa Rica (1,273) Colombia (1,707) Mexico (1,971) Peru (1,731)	cross-tabular	(F) direct (H) direct
World Fertility Survey (1976)	Nepal (5,665)	cross-tabular	(F) direct

Note: (F)= education of women; (M) = education of men; (H) = husband's education of women.
a. Statistically significant.
Sources: For complete references, see the sources for this chapter.

The importance of education in contraceptive knowledge

What causes the effect of education on contraceptive knowledge to differ from place to place? If this question could be answered it might be possible to determine whether it is education itself or some other variables that cause differences in contraceptive knowledge—such as urban residence, mass media exposure, and income. Only if such questions can be answered can education be considered an appropriate policy instrument. Some light can be shed on this issue. Fortunately, both the CELADE and Value of Children studies include the many factors affecting contraceptive knowledge in the same analysis.

The Value of Children survey (Arnold, 1975) used several socio-economic variables and many value indexes to explain contraceptive knowledge. The socioeconomic variables of interest are age, income, education, urban experience, media exposure, and marriage duration. Education was significantly positively related to knowledge in all cases even when these other variables were controlled. However, its relative importance in explaining knowledge varied. In Hawaii, the Philippines, and Thailand it was the most important variable. In Korea education ranked below media exposure and age. In Taiwan it ranked below media exposure. In Japan it ranked below media exposure and urban experience. Media exposure thus seemed to be the major alternative factor explaining contraceptive knowledge and was significantly positive in all cases and second to education in the Philippines and Thailand. The mass media effect was stronger in countries with strong family planning programs, indicating that mass media can possibly be a substitute for formal education, but the latter continues to have a strong effect even in those circumstances.[5]

In the CELADE study (1972), the partial correlations for education were significant everywhere and rank first in all cities except Bogotá, San Jose, and Caracas, where they ranked sixth, fifth, and fourth, respectively. The number of living children also had consistently significant correlations in all cities and ranked higher than education in Bogotá, San Jose, and Caracas. Family expenditures, a substitute for family income, was significantly positive in all cities except Rio de Janeiro and ranked first or second in five of the cities. This indicates the importance of income in providing access to knowledge in countries that had neither official nor private family planning programs. In the early 1960s none of these Latin American countries had such programs.

Thus, education has a significant effect on contraceptive knowledge in countries with and without family planning programs even after controlling for many other variables. The major limitation on the information available is the small number of studies in Africa and the limited number of published studies of rural as opposed to urban populations.

---

5. Part of the effect of education may be disguised in these results, since education probably increases media exposure—at least exposure to printed media. The zero-order correlations between education and knowledge were by far the largest of all variables except in Japan.

The community level of education and contraceptive knowledge

In a recent unpublished paper using the rural Latin American sample surveys, Simmons and de Jong have attempted to determine whether the level of education in the general community interacts with the wife's level of schooling to determine contraceptive knowledge. They found that the community's level of education was important in determining the percentage of women who knew about contraception even when the individual's level of education was controlled. In particular, in areas where there was the least knowledge of contraception (Peru), the community level of education rivaled the individual's level of education in explaining contraceptive knowledge.[6] This relation may explain in part the interaction between communal level of education and individual education in the education-completed fertility relation observed in Chapter 1. It would be useful to know whether this phenomena is peculiar to rural areas and unique to countries that lack broad family planning programs.

Communication between Husband and Wife

There is some evidence that communication between husband and wife increases contraceptive use and reduces fertility (Mitchell, 1972; Michel, 1967; Hill and others, 1959; Ramakumar and Gopal, 1972; and Simmons and Culagovski, 1973).[7] There is also some evidence that education increases the level of husband-wife communications, as summarized in Table 5.3. This evidence is not extensive, but what there is shows a direct relation between education and level of communication. The study by Mukherjee (1975) is the most detailed of those cited and contains data from three areas of India divided into urban and rural samples. Number of communication media used, frequency of radio listening, literacy, wife's education, and husband's education were all generally directly related to frequency of husband-wife communication, and the strength of the correlations was in the

6. It is not possible from the study cited to determine why the community level of education has the effect it does.

7. Mukherjee also showed that husband-wife communication was positively correlated in a significant manner with knowledge of and attitude toward family planning.

Table 5.3. *Evidence on Education and Communication between Husband and Wife*

Study (date published)	Location (sample size)	Method	Direction of relation
Brody and others (1977)	Jamaica (150)	correlation	(F) direct
Khalifa (1976)	Egypt—rural (1973) (1,234)	cross-tabular	(F) direct
Mukherjee (1975)	India	zero-order correlation	(F) education—direct[a] (H) education—direct[a] (F) literacy—direct[b] number of communication media used—direct[d] frequency of radio listening—direct[e]
Olusanya (1971)	Western Nigeria (1966) (4,408)	cross-tabular	(F) direct (M) direct
Oppong (1970)	Accra, Ghana (1967–68) (163)	cross-tabular	(F) direct
Pool (1970)	Ghana (1965–66) (5,700)	cross-tabular	(F) direct
Ramakumar and Gopal (1972)	India (534)	cross-tabular	(F) direct

Note: (M) = education of men; (F) = education of women; (H) = husband's education of women.
  a. Statistically significant in one case.
  b. Statistically significant in three cases.
  c. Statistically significant in five of six cases.
  d. Statistically significant in all cases.
Sources: For complete references, see the sources for this chapter.

order listed. Thus husband-wife communication seems to be related to level of communication in general more than to education itself. Some unsolved issues related to this variable exist. The relative importance of the husband's and wife's education is perhaps the most critical unsolved question.

Contraceptive Use

Behavior—as opposed to attitudes, opinions, or knowledge—needs to be considered in the context of the individual's external circumstances. Thus the relation between actual fertility and education needs to be examined in the context of the age or length of marriage for the woman, although desired or ideal family size can at least theoretically be considered independently of those variables. Likewise, attitudes toward and knowledge of different methods of contraception can be examined for women of any age or marital status, but whether a woman actually uses contraception or has used it in the past depends so much on her age, her number of births, and the duration of her marriage that examination of use that does not control for at least one of these factors is likely to generate highly spurious results. Therefore, the relation between education and contraceptive use will be examined only where age, number of births, or marital duration are used as controls.

Table 5.4 summarizes the results of studies in Latin America, Asia, and the Middle East. Unfortunately, no studies of contraceptive use with the appropriate age controls could be found for Africa. In Latin America both the CELADE (1972) and other studies show direct relations between education of women and use of contraception even after controlling for other factors. In all cities except Panama City, the coefficients of education are significant. The coefficient of the husband's education is significant only in Panama City and Bogotá. Thus the wife's education seems to be more important than that of her husband in determining contraceptive use.

Asia is represented by studies of Korea (Chung and others, 1972), Taiwan (Speare and others, 1973), Thailand (Knodel and Pitakepsombati, 1973), West Malaysia (Palmore, 1969), and Nepal (WFS, 1977). The Taiwan and Korean studies show direct relations as do the rural Thai and urban West Malaysian sample. In urban Thailand, however, women with 1 to 3 years of schooling exhibit the lowest contraceptive use rather than those with no education.[8] In rural West

8. The 1976 World Fertility Survey in Thailand showed a uniformly direct relation between education and contraceptive use overall, but for women under 25, those with no education had slightly higher previous usage than those with 1 to 4 years of schooling.

Table 5.4. *Evidence on Education and the Use of Birth Control*

Study (date published)	Location (sample size)	Method	Direction of relation
CELADE (1972)	9 Latin American cities (1964–65)	multiple correlation (see Table 1.5)	(F) direct[a]—except Panama City (H) direct[a]—only Panama City and Bogotá
Chung and others (1972)	Korea (1971)	cross-tabular	(F) direct[a]
Khalifa (1976)	Cairo, Egypt (1970) (569)	cross-tabular	(F) direct (M) curvilinear
Knodel and Pitakepsombati (1973)	Thailand (1969–70) (3,500)	cross-tabular	(F) rural—direct urban—lower use with 4 years than less educated
Palmore (1969)	West Malaysia (1966–67) (5,457)	cross-tabular	(F) metropolitan— direct other urban—direct rural—no difference
Sear (1975)	Cali, Colombia (1973) (508)	multiple regression	(F) direct[a]
Speare and others (1973)	Taiwan (3,579)	multiple classification analysis	(F) direct
World Fertility Survey (1977)	Nepal (5,665)	cross-tabular	(F) direct (H) direct
Yaukey (1963)	Lebanon (613)	cross-tabular	(F) urban—direct

Note: Age, parity, or marital duration are controlled for. (F) = education of women; (M) = education of men; (H) = husband's education of women.
a. Statistically significant.
Sources: For complete references, see the sources for this chapter.

Malaysia there is no difference in use by education. The only other deviation from a strictly direct relation is found for males in Egypt (Khalifa, 1976), where those with a middle level of education among wives over 45 have the highest contraceptive use. But given the relatively small sample size, these differences are of questionable significance. In Lebanon (Yaukey, 1963), education is directly related to both past use of abortion and contraception among Moslems and Christians in urban areas. Thus, as is the case with the relation between education and the other fertility regulation variables, the relation for contraceptive use is almost uniformly direct. It is certainly more uniform than is the relation between actual fertility and education and appears to be even more consistent than the relation between education and age of marriage, since there are no differences such as the East-West patterns observed by Dixon.

Details of the relation

The size of the effect of education on contraceptive use can be seen in Table 5.5, which is taken from the Freedman and Coombs cross-cultural study (1974). The data come primarily from Asian countries, although one Latin American and one Middle Eastern country are represented. No African data are presented. Table 5.6 summarizes west African studies (Caldwell, 1975) on the relation between education and contraceptive use. With two exceptions these show a direct relation between use and education. However, these studies do not control for age, number of births, or marital duration.

In Table 5.5 there are two countries that do not show a uniformly direct relation between education and contraceptive usage—Korea and urban Thailand. In Table 5.4 urban Thailand showed curvilinear relation, with those with 4 years of schooling showing lowest use. This does not show up in Table 5.5, perhaps because of the aggregation over all levels of primary school, but there is a slight irregularity in an otherwise uniformly inverse relation for those who achieved senior high school. The Korean result conflicts with the data presented by Chung and others (1972), cited in Table 5.4. The difference in Korea probably results from the fact that Chung and others cited data on whether a woman had ever used contraception or abortion, but the Freedman and Coombs data are on current use of contraception. Since the most educated women in Korea have high abortion use, they would be expected to rely less on contraception.[9]

Table 5.5 also shows the wide variety of levels of contraceptive use. Among women 30 to 39 the use rate ranges from 11 percent in West

---

9. Of women with four or more live births who have at least high school education, 59 percent have used abortion.

Table 5.5. *Percentage Currently Using Contraception for Married Women 20 to 39 Years Old, by Wife's Age and Education*

Wife's age (years) and education	Ankara[a] 1966	Calcutta 1970	India 1970	Korea 1971	West Malaysia 1966–67	West Malaysia 1970	Mexico City 1971	Philippines 1968	Taiwan 1967	Taiwan[b] 1970	Thailand (urban) 1970	Thailand (rural) 1969
20 to 29	42	38	10	10	7	17	23	16	16	26	34	9
No formal	18	18	5	12	2	11	2	9	12	21	18	0
Primary	38	38	18	10	7	17	20	14	16	22	33	10
Junior high	41	37	—[d]	6	12	26	41	20	26	48	43	—[c]
Senior high and over	68	65	30	14	33	30	—[c]	29	36	49	37	—[c]
30 to 39	41	43	15	33	11	19	25	18	45	58	48	16
No formal	26	23	10	22	5	13	8	11	37	51	33	9
Primary	50	51	21	36	17	23	21	15	48	61	50	17
Junior high	61	60	—[d]	41	36	36	51	22	66	72	57	—[c]
Senior high and over	62	66	46	39	49	47	—[c]	34	70	81	55	—[c]

20 to 39	37	40	12	24	9	18	24	17	32	44	42	13
No formal	22	21	8	20	4	12	5	10	26	39	30	6
Primary	43	44	19	24	11	19	21	15	33	43	43	14
Junior high	53	47	—d	24	23	29	45	21	45	60	50	—c
Senior high and over	65	65	36	26	39	36	47	32	51	63	47	—c
Sample size	552	947	10,246	1,620	4,242	13,449	486	25,604e	4,300	2,491	1,080	642

Note: See Appendix 1, item 6 of source for definitions. Sterilization included as contraception except in Belgium and Great Britain.

a. Defined as, ever used contraception.

b. Taiwan 1970 data refer to ages 22 to 39.

c. Less than 20 cases in the category.

d. No such category.

e. Frequency is weighted as follows: urban respondents × 4 and rural respondents × 12.

Source: R. Freedman and L. Coombs, *Cross-Cultural Comparisons: Data on Two Factors in Fertility Behavior* (New York: The Population Council, 1974).

Table 5.6. *Percentage Using Contraception in West Africa, by Various Measures of Education*

Study	Location	Year	Sex	Information	Highest level of education reached				
					No schooling	Elementary	Middle school[a]	Secondary	Tertiary[b]
Ohadike	Lagos	1964	F	ever used any contraception	5	8	—	20	71
				ever used modern contraception	1	3	—	17	50
Okediji	Ibadan	1965–6	F	ever used any contraception	11	17	10	36	85
				ever used modern contraception	0	0	2	27	58
Igun, Olusanya, and Acsadi	Irrua (rural Nigeria)	1970	F	ever used any contraception	2	5	—	5	—[c]
Caldwell and Igun	Lagos	1969	M and F	ever used modern contraception	10		22		
Caldwell and Igun	Southern Nigeria (urban)[d]	1969	M and F	ever used modern contraception	2		14		
Caldwell and Igun	Northern Nigeria (urban)[e]	1969	M and F	ever used modern contraception	0.7[f]		1.3[f]		
Caldwell and Igun	Nigeria (rural)[g]	1969	M and F	ever used modern contraception	0.04[f]		1.9[f]		

Dow	Freetown	1969–70	F	ever used any contraception	12		29
Dow	Sierra Leone (other urban)	1969–70	F	ever used any contraception	9		20
Dow	Sierra Leone (rural)	1969–70	F	ever used any contraception	3		16
Caldwell	Ghana (urban elite)	1963	F	ever used any contraception		27	44
				currently using contraception		20	36
Caldwell	Ghana (urban elite)	1963	M	ever used any contraception		24	41
				currently using modern contraception		20	36

Joint education of husband and wife

					Neither with any education	Wife only with some education	Husband only with some education	Both with some education
Ohadike	Lagos	1964	F	ever used modern contraception	0	0	2	9
Dow	Freetown	1969–70	F	ever used any contraception	11	24	10	31

(Table continues on the following page)

Table 5.6 (continued)

Study	Location	Year	Sex	Information	Literacy		Level of information[h]	
					Illiterate	Literate	Low	High
Dow	Sierra Leone (other urban)	1969–70	F	ever used any contraception	8	20	8	23
Dow	Sierra Leone (rural)	1960–70	F	ever used any contraception	3	12	3	18

Note: These studies do not control for age or marital duration.

a. In some ex-British colonies, this is a postprimary or postelementary school to improve educational standards for admission to secondary schools.

b. All further education requiring at least some secondary schooling or incorporating it.

c. Numbers too low to be significant.

d. Western and Kwara states.

e. Kano.

f. Decimal parts of percentages are given because of the very small numbers.

g. Western, Kwara, and Kano states.

h. Measured by a standardized series of questions on various subjects.

Source: Caldwell, John C. (ed.), *Population Growth and Socio-Economic Change in West Africa* (New York: Columbia University Press, 1975), Table 3.6. Sources cited in this table can be found in Caldwell (1975) but not in the sources to this chapter.

Malaysia in 1966–67 to 58 percent in Taiwan in 1970. The differences across educational groups range from 8 percent in rural Thailand to 44 percent in West Malaysia in 1966–67. Differences are somewhat larger in cities and urban areas than for countries as a whole. This can be seen by comparing Calcutta and India in 1970. The differences for Ankara and Mexico City are both fairly large. Differences in use also appear to narrow over time. They narrowed substantially in West Malaysia between 1966–67 and 1970 and somewhat less in Taiwan between those years.

It would be difficult to say what increment in education has the greatest impact on contraceptive use. In Ankara, Calcutta, Korea, and urban Thailand, the step from no education to primary education had the greatest impact. In West Malaysia, Mexico City, and Taiwan in 1967 it was the step from primary to secondary school. In the Philippines it was the step from junior to senior high school which had the greatest impact.

Reasons for direct relation

Contraceptive use should increase with education for several reasons. First, the more educated appear to have greater natural fertility and generally higher rates of survival for their children. Second, ideal and desired family size tend to be inversely related to education. Third, the more educated have better attitudes toward and knowledge of contraception. Fourth, more educated people tend to be more rational in their behavior: that is, if they do not want more children, they will do something to prevent more births. The first three reasons have already been discussed. Freedman and Coombs (1974) give some evidence on the fourth point by showing the proportions of women in each educational group who do not want more children and who are not using contraception.[10] These data are presented in Table 5.7.

The proportion of women who do not want more children and do

10. Women who do not want more children may not use contraception for several reasons: they may no longer be fertile; they may be able to rely on abortion; contraception may be unavailable or available at high cost. Alternatively where women have little freedom or control over their own lives, they may not have access to contraception because of husband's restrictions. See Goldberg and Litton (1967) on this concept of access.

not use contraception ranges from 29 percent in Delhi to 89 percent in Jakarta. This probably reflects the availability of contraception in Jakarta at the time of the survey. However, high rates (80 percent or more) of nonuse were also found in rural Thailand in 1969–70, the Philippines, West Malaysia, and India. The effect of education on nonuse for this group is inverse, as expected in all cases except Korea, where reliance on abortion is a popular alternative. The differences across educational groups range from a low of 12 percent in rural Thailand, where differences between only two education groups were studied, to a high over 50 percent in West Malaysia and Mexico City.

As in the case of overall contraceptive usage, the level of education with the greatest impact on use differs from study to study. The difference in use between those with no schooling and those with primary schooling is greatest in Ankara, Calcutta, Delhi, Korea, and urban Thailand. The step from primary to junior high levels has the greatest impact in West Malaysia, Mexico City, and Taiwan. These patterns are the same for current use. In Jakarta the largest difference occurs between junior and senior high schools.

This information on contraceptive use is impressive in the uniformity of its relation to education. Unfortunately, the variation in differences by educational levels is so great that statements cannot be made about which level of education should be emphasized. Another problem is that it is impossible to determine the extent to which the effect of education on use results from its effect on motivation (through its effects on the supply of and demand for children) and how much results from its effect on access to contraception through more knowledge, high incomes, urban residence, and better medical care.

Some insight into these problems can be obtained from Table 5.8, which shows the variables that were significant in explaining contraceptive use in multiple correlation analysis of the CELADE data. The variables included here are not only objective measures such as age, income, and education but also subjective variables such as desired family size, contraceptive attitudes, and so forth. The wife's education was not significant when these intervening knowledge, attitude, and motivation variables were controlled. Knowledge of contraception was the most important explanatory variable. The desire for more children was also significant in all cities. Level of motivation and attitude toward family planning were next in importance, followed by an index of religiousness and desired family size. It has been shown that education acts on knowledge, attitude, and desired family size. Expenditures by the family (which substitutes for income) and the husband's education are only significant in three and two countries, respectively. Thus these results indicate that the major effects of the wife's education are those acting through contraceptive knowledge and attitude and desired family size[11] rather than through family income, even in an environment where there were few public family planning programs.

Mueller and Cohn's study (1977) of males in Taiwan gives an example of the factors explaining contraceptive use in an environment where they are extensively provided to the public. This shows that the relative importance of education on contraceptive use depended on which other variables were included in the analysis. The effect of education was reduced most dramatically when media exposure was included in the analysis. In that case, only the wife's age surpassed media exposure, and the effect of the wife's education tied with cost sensitivity and the perceived utility of children in importance. The husband's education was even less important.

Summary

The relation between education and all the fertility regulation variables is the most direct and consistent observed in this study. There are very few deviations from the expected pattern. In Latin America, even Buenos Aires has the expected relations although not all of them are statistically significant. Only Thailand appears to be anomalous, and even here contraceptive knowledge, although not monotonically related to education, does have a significantly positive regression coefficient. Nonmetropolitan West Malaysia was atypical with respect to attitudes, but not to knowledge.

In general, education increases contraceptive knowledge in a stronger and more uniform manner than it improves attitudes toward contraception. In addition, scarce evidence shows that education uniformly increases communication between husband and wife. Edu-

---

11. Evidence on use in Table 5.4 is obtained from multiple correlations which did not include the intervening variables of knowledge, attitude, motivation, or desired family size. In those calculations education did have a significant effect.

Table 5.7. Percentage Not Using Contraception of Those Who Want No More Children, for Married Women 20 to 39 Years Old, by Wife's Age and Education

Wife's age (years) and education	Ankara[a] 1966	Calcutta 1970	Delhi 1968–69	India 1970	Jakarta 1968	Korea 1971	West Malaysia 1966–67	Mexico City 1971	Philippines 1968	Taiwan 1967	Taiwan[b] 1970	Thailand (urban) 1970	Thailand (rural) 1969
20 to 29	64	48	33	80	89	73	87	68	84	56	45	49	87
No formal	79	59	56	89	100	78	92	—[c]	95	63	53	—[c]	—[c]
Primary	53	—[c]	23	67	92	66	87	73	87	56	48	51	86
Junior high	—[c]	52	15	—[d]	78	85	—[c]	—[c]	74	39	16	45	—[c]
Senior high and over	—[c]	26	12	54	67	—[c]	—[c]	—[c]	69	28	11	—[c]	—[c]
30 to 39	53	49	27	80	89	58	80	75	82	45	33	39	88
No formal	65	68	44	35	95	72	89	92	96	54	42	54	94
Primary	45	44	19	77	89	53	72	77	85	42	31	36	87
Junior high	38	37	10	—[d]	89	47	43	44	76	26	17	31	—[c]

Senior high and over	—c	23	7	46	45	45	32	—c	62	21	6	30	—c
20 to 39	58	49	29	80	89	60	82	72	83	47	36	41	88
No formal	71	65	48	86	97	73	89	93	95	56	44	56	96
Primary	49	45	20	73	91	55	77	75	86	45	35	40	87
Junior high	41	43	11	—d	80	56	54	39	75	30	17	36	—c
Senior high and over	23	26	9	49	61	52	37	—c	64	23	8	23	—c
Sample size[e]	310	511	3,009	5,195	367	795	1,302	234	13,776[f]	2,313	1,521	543	370

Note: See Appendix 1, items 3 and 6 of source for definitions. Sterilization included as contraception except in Belgium and Great Britain.

a. Defined as of those wanting no more children, percent never used contraception.
b. Taiwan 1970 data refer to ages 22 to 39.
c. Less than 20 cases in the category.
d. No such category.
e. Sample size based only on the women who want no more children.
f. Frequency is weighted as follows: urban respondents × 4 and rural respondents × 12.

Source: R. Freedman and L. Coombs, *Cross Cultural Comparisons: Data on Two Factors in Fertility Behavior* (New York: The Population Council, 1974).

Table 5.8. *Multiple Correlations between the Index of the Use of Contraception and Sets of Explanatory Variables with Significant Partial Correlations from a Thirty-seven Variable Regression Analysis*

Variable	Location							Ecuador	
	Buenos Aires	Rio de Janeiro	Bogotá	San Jose	Mexico City	Panama City	Caracas	Quito	Guayaquil
Multiple correlation coefficients (R)									
Total, 37 variables, all categories	0.408	0.487	0.637	0.553	0.609	0.536	0.535	0.592	0.570
Sociodemographic variables (13)	0.213	0.285	0.450	0.372	0.376	0.333	0.362	0.387	0.367
Social psychological variables (7)	0.343	0.463	0.606	0.504	0.597	0.495	0.503	0.555	0.529
Ideals of reproduction variables (5)	0.144	0.101	0.145	0.131	0.167	0.070	0.174	0.072	0.106
Religiosity variables (2)	0.123	0.067	0.136	0.156	0.082	0.035	0.061	0.155	0.060
Family structure variables (3)	0.040	0.056	0.081	0.080	0.132	0.128	0.174	0.069	0.120
Modernization variables (6)	0.132	0.209	0.375	0.268	0.264	0.207	0.291	0.290	0.247
Significant partial correlations									
Index of contraceptive knowledge	0.263	0.340	0.407	0.334	0.445	0.386	0.330	0.412	0.402
Index: couple desire for more children	−0.088	−0.069	−0.128	−0.112	−0.061	−0.163	−0.104	−0.063	−0.084
Motivation index	−0.076	−0.105	−0.071	−0.107	−0.071	−0.076	−0.086		−0.094
Index: attitude toward family planning	0.116		0.059	0.073			0.067	0.088	

Frequency of communion	0.072							0.113
Ideal family size—self			0.110	0.059			−0.062	0.130
Expenditures of the family		0.058	0.083	0.086	0.094			
Fear of child mortality	0.055		0.072	0.060				0.053
Ideal interval—marriage to first child	0.057			0.089	−0.070			
Educational attainment of husband			0.051		0.055			
Magazine reading							0.067	0.063
Authority structure in family	0.055			0.071				
Index: companionship in marriage				0.051				
Index: self-referral					−0.075			0.081
Place of birth of husband					−0.074			
Ideal interval between births					0.062			
Index: legitimacy (religious stand) with respect to family planning						0.098		
Ideal age to have last child						−0.074		
Marital status						−0.062	0.095	
Social mobility aspiration for son							0.075	
Frequency of attendance religious services								
Employment status of respondent							−0.058	
Social mobility aspiration for daughter							−0.054	
Additional education of the couple							−0.052	

Source: CELADE and CFSC, *Fertility and Family Planning in Metropolitan Latin America* (Chicago: University of Chicago, 1972) p. 249.

cation increases contraceptive use, but this relation is slightly less uniform than that for contraceptive knowledge.

Both mass media exposure and education are important in explaining knowledge of contraceptive methods in countries with public family planning programs. Even in these cases, however, education continues to have strong effects, and where there are (or were) no such programs, it is even more important.

The CELADE study indicates that the effect of education on contraceptive use acts through its effects on knowledge, attitude, and motivation and perhaps to a lesser extent on access to family planning through higher income in Latin American cities. It is these multiple channels of effects, all in the same direction, that explain why the relation between contraceptive use and education is so uniformly strong.

The fact that education is uniformly related to contraceptive use, but not uniformly related to completed fertility may appear paradoxical. However, the literature does not show that contraceptive users systematically have smaller families. They often have larger families. In circumstances where desired family size exceeds natural fertility, education may be associated with higher natural fertility and higher actual fertility. At the same time, only those with higher education and fertility that equals or exceeds desired fertility may be motivated to use contraception.

6

•-•-

Summary and Implications

Both theoretical and empirical evidence indicate that education in the poorest regions may increase the ability to conceive and carry conceptions to successful live births. In the short run, this increase would tend to increase actual fertility. In the long run, however, the positive initial effect of education on fertility may become negative. This reversal occurs in part simply as a result of recognizing the increased ability to have live births and the survival of those births. This recognition and the adjustment to new conditions take time, and this time lag explains why fertility often rises before it begins to fall (Leibenstein, 1977). In this chapter the empirical evidence and the theoretical model supporting the above conclusion are summarized, and the research and policy implications of the results are discussed.

Summary

Several recent reviews on the determinants of fertility have concluded that the inverse relation between education and fertility is one of the most consistent and best documented in the literature.

Such statements tempt policymakers to use educational policies to speed the reduction of fertility. The fairly extensive review of the evidence in this study, however, shows that the relation between education and fertility is not always inverse. The earlier generalizations about such a relation probably resulted from a scarcity of data in the poorest, least literate societies and in rural areas where the inverse relation is less likely to occur.

Aggregate and individual studies

Population policy is concerned with the rate of population growth and thus with aggregate levels of fertility as measured by crude birth rates. Therefore, from a policy perspective the relation between the aggregate level of education in a country and the crude birth rate is of greatest interest. Such aggregate relations are almost invariably inverse when countries with different educational levels are compared. The factors causing such relations are, however, highly uncertain given the many other factors that are associated with various education levels. If the age structure of the population and the level of income are controlled, then statistically significant inverse relations are only observed in less than 60 percent of the cases. In addition, when cross-regional data from within developing countries are used and the age structure and extent of urbanization is controlled, there are statistically significant inverse relations in less than 60 percent of the cases, and in some cases significantly positive relations are observed. These aggregate data tend to indicate that inverse relations are less likely in the least developed countries. Unfortunately, given the lack of well-developed national statistical systems in the poorest countries, it is impossible to find enough aggregate studies relating education and fertility in these countries.

To explore the relation of education and fertility further, studies on the individual level can be examined. Such studies can be based on sample surveys that are too small or too localized to provide cross-regional comparisons. Two kinds of cross-individual studies of the relation in developing countries are reviewed: those simply comparing the fertility (adjusted for age) of individuals with different levels of education and multiple regression studies in which fertility is explained using education and income as two of the explanatory variables and introducing a control for age. The first kind of study shows an inverse relation (not necessarily significant) in 49 percent of the cases; the second type shows an inverse relation in about 58 percent of the cases.

These aggregate percentages are somewhat irrelevant. The overall rate depends on what subgroups are studied because of great differences revealed in both kinds of studies in the relation in different subgroups. Both kinds of studies show that: (a) female education is more likely to be inversely related than male education; (b) education in urban areas is more likely to be inversely related than in rural areas; and (c) education in countries with literacy rates above 40 percent is more likely to be inversely related than in less literate countries. Thus, the overall percentage of inverse relations depends very much on the distribution of studies in various categories.

Thus the data seem to show a definite pattern of nonlinearity. In the least-developed countries, small amounts of education are associated with higher fertility, but larger amounts are associated with lower fertility. In general, however, there are much fewer studies of rural than urban areas, of males than females, and in less literate than more literate societies. In addition, the studies in the least literate societies are more likely to be based on very small sample sizes. It is expected that the World Fertility Survey will correct this imbalance and will provide a much firmer empirical base for generalizations about fertility at various levels of development. Unfortunately, these surveys, like many of those cited earlier, are restricted to women who have been married and thus may tend to understate the total effect of education on fertility if education increases the proportion of women who never marry.

Model of education and fertility

The simple replication of studies relating education and fertility in a wider variety of countries with fairly uniform data will help to clarify the situations in which education is inversely related to fertility. Such studies, however, will not clarify how education affects fertility. A model is needed to establish whether the observed association between the variables is in fact causal. In addition, such a model must explain why education affects fertility differently in different situations.

An attempt was made to develop such a model in Chapter 2. That model was based on the premise that education does not affect fertility directly but acts through many variables that in turn determine fertility. First, the evidence relating these intervening variables to fertility was reviewed, and then the relation of education to these intervening variables was reviewed. A simplified version of that model is presented in Figure 6.1. This model traces the impact of education on fertility through the intervening variables determining fertility. The evidence reviewed on the relation between education and the intervening variables is summarized in Table 6.1.

Fertility is determined by three factors: the biological supply of children, the demand for children, and the regulation of fertility. Each of these factors is in turn influenced directly by many variables, as shown in Figure 2.2, and indirectly by education, as shown in Figure 6.1.[1] The model represents a situation in which the current number of living children is compared with the demand for children. If that number equals or exceeds demand, then it is possible that fertility will be regulated to limit further births. Whether regulation is in fact used, however, also depends on the desired family size of husbands and wives; whether they communicate with each other; the relative power of each spouse in decisionmaking; and attitudes toward, knowledge of, and access to contraception. Thus, the effect of education on fertility depends on how education affects the three factors that determine fertility: the supply of children, the demand for children, and fertility regulation. Given the multiple channels through which education affects fertility, it is hardly surprising that its effect is not uniformly inverse.

Data on education and the determinants of fertility

Table 6.1 summarizes the data on the relation of education to the intervening variables and the consequent probable effect of education through these variables on fertility and completed family size. The indirect effects in the third column of Table 6.1 are shown in Figure 6.1. Table 6.1 and Figure 6.1 show that education tends to reduce the demand for children, as measured by desired family size, by reducing preferences for and perceived benefits of children. Education, particularly the husband's education, however, also tends to increase the perceived ability to afford children. This tendency counters the negative effects to some extent but does not outweigh them, since

1. This model shows only the major blocks of variables contained in Figure 2.2 but adds the education of husband and wife and its impact on the intervening variables to the fertility model of Chapter 2.

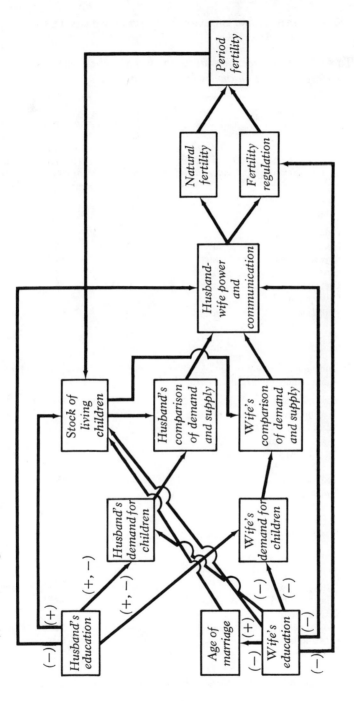

Figure 6.1. Model of the Effect of Education on Fertility through the Major Intervening Variables

Table 6.1. *Evidence Supporting the Relation between Education and Fertility through the Intervening Variables*

Variable	Relation of education and variable	Probable relation of education through the variable	Results Supporting (number of cases)	Results Not supporting (number of cases)
Potential supply of births	?	?	—	—
Probability of marrying	inverse	—	6	5[a]
Age of marriage	direct	—	59	12[a]
Health	direct	+	2	0
Lactation	inverse	+	6	0
Postpartum abstinence	inverse	+	2	0
Infant or child mortality	inverse	—	16	7
Demand for children (desired family size)	inverse	—	17	8[a]
Preference for children	inverse			
Ideal family size		—	20	7[a]
Desired number of sons		—	8	1
Perceived benefits of children	inverse	—	17	2
Perceived costs of children	direct	—	2	0
Perceived ability to afford children	direct	+	9	3
Fertility regulation (contraceptive use)	direct	—	26	11
Attitudes toward birth control	direct	—	28	4
Knowledge of birth control	direct	—	28	1
Husband-wife communication	direct	—	9	0

a. Relation of male education to the variable is much weaker than that of female education.

desired family size is generally negatively related to fertility. Education also reduces the number of births needed to achieve a particular desired family size by lowering infant and child mortality. The evidence is also very strong that education increases contraceptive use by improving attitudes toward, and knowledge of, contraception.

Education has multiple, partially offsetting effects on the potential biological supply of births or fecundity. In those countries with the poorest health and nutrition combined with traditional reliance on contraceptive practices such as lactation and postpartum abstinence, education would be most likely to have a strong positive effect on fecundity.

The most immediate factor countering this increase in fecundity is probably the effect of education on the age of marriage. Female education seems to reduce the years married by raising the age of marriage and, at least in some countries, by reducing the probability of marriage. If the marriage age is very young, however, raising that age by a year or so may have little effect on fertility, since few very young women give birth because of the high incidence of adolescent sterility. Only when the age of marriage is in the late teens can further delays in the age of marriage be expected to reduce fertility.

The effect of education on the fecundity of married women, however, appears to operate in a different direction by improving the health of women sufficiently to increase their chances of conceiving and their ability to carry births to term. In addition, more educated women tend to give up traditional behavior such as prolonged lactation and postpartum abstinence which tend to suppress fertility.

Increased fecundity can, of course, be offset by increased contraceptive use, but there are very good reasons for expecting contraception use to lag behind the increase in fecundity. The supply of births and the survival rate must first increase more than the increase in demand resulting from a greater ability to afford children. Once this point has been reached, individuals will need time to adapt to the new condition or, even in some cases, to understand that the changes necessitate changes in behavior. Since the more educated tend to perceive changes in their environment more accurately (for example, changes in child mortality), education should reduce the adjustment lag.

Therefore, the effect of education on fertility through the intervening variables tends to be negative except for possible effects through natural fertility (through biological and behavioral factors) and the ability to afford children. These positive effects appear to be stronger as a consequence of the husband's education than of the wife's education.

Implications for Further Research

This review suggests that several kinds of research are needed to clarify these issues. First, more studies need to be done relating education and age-adjusted fertility in certain under-researched areas. Second, the effect of education on several variables that are important in determining fertility has not been studied sufficiently. Third, little or no work has been done to determine which of the various aspects of the education process are most important in reducing fertility. Fourth, the model presented above needs to be tested in its entirety to determine the relative importance of the many channels through which education affects fertility.

More work in under-researched areas

There is not enough research relating the age-adjusted fertility and the education of individuals in the poorest countries and in rural areas within most countries. In addition, not enough work has explored the relation of education and fertility for males. The World Fertility Survey should provide the data needed for such studies in the poorest countries and in rural areas. In addition it will provide data on the husband's level of education and its effect on actual fertility and the wife's attitudes, but only a few of the WFS studies will interview husbands about their own attitudes. Such studies will help to establish if the patterns described in this review are correct.

Explanation of observed patterns

More research is needed to understand why these different patterns are observed. The simplest kind of work should examine the effect of education on the intervening variables separately for men and women in urban and rural areas. The most important variables that need to be examined in this detail are age of marriage, ideal and desired family size, the biological supply of children, and contraceptive knowledge and attitude. It is expected that such research will result in several conclusions.

(a) If a large part of the effect of female education on age of marriage results from the opening up of attractive, well paying jobs that are not compatible with marriage, then female education will probably have little effect on age of marriage of those in the rural areas where such jobs do not exist. Education, however, may raise the overall age of marriage of the country, even in the rural areas, by encouraging migration of educated women to the urban areas where such jobs are available.

(b) Education may have different effects on ideal and desired family size in urban and rural areas because the costs and benefits of children may differ in these circumstances.

(c) The fertility regulation variables showed very consistent relations with education, but these data were generally not broken down by urban or rural residence. The differences in contraceptive use between those with various levels of education tended to be larger for cities than for whole countries, but this is highly tentative.

(d) In addition to fairly simple comparisons of the links of education to intervening variables, more complex forms of research are needed. The effect of education on the biological supply of children is not well understood. More research is needed on finding measures of fecundity and relating these to education. Education of males and females may have different effects on health and thus on the potential supply of births and children. Education may improve health through access to medical care and better nutrition given by higher income. If this is the case, male education may have stronger effects on the supply of children than female education. Alternatively, education may affect health by giving individuals better knowledge of good health and nutrition practices; here, female education may be more important.

Different effects of factors

For the relation between fertility and education to generate policy implications, it is necessary to know not only the extent to which other factors can substitute for the effect of education, but also what characteristics of education decrease fertility. It may be that education itself has no effect, but that the educational system selects out individuals with certain background characteristics—for example, intelligence, ambition, and high socioeconomic status—and these characteristics may lead to lower fertility even if higher education were not obtained. Alternatively, education may provide explicit skills, such as literacy and numeracy, which result in lower fertility either through better job opportunities or through improved abilities to acquire new information and to use complicated technologies. Education may primarily change attitudes, resulting in more modern attitudes toward the control of one's life, the possibilities of social mobility, or the proper roles of men and women. Education may provide explicit knowledge that will result in lower fertility. Finally, education, particularly secondary education, may serve as a simple alternative to early marriage in societies where there are very few alternatives. These various effects of education were sketched in Figure 1.1. The most important relations that need to be explored are those between: (a) female education, market opportunities, and women's wages and fertility and age of marriage; and (b) education and fertility regulation.

Although much work has been done on female labor participation and fertility, both positive and negative relations have been shown. In addition, it has been shown that while female labor participation increases the age of marriage and proportion of women never married in Eastern Europe, the Middle East, and Asia, it has no such effect in Western Europe and English overseas areas.[2] Both of these factors suggest that it is not simply labor participation that must be considered, but the compatibility of work with marriage and childbearing and the wages in that work. Compatibility of work and marriage or childbearing depends on many factors: social definitions of appropriate roles, location of work, rigidity of hours, cost of child care, availability of contraceptives, and so forth. Wages are important because economic models suggest that fertility, marriage, and labor supply are jointly determined by the wife's market wage. Both the effect of education on wages and on the compatibility of work and family roles and the effect of these variables on fertility need to be explored more fully. One possible explanation of the interaction between the individual's level of education and the aggregate level of literacy and fertility is that as long as overall female literacy or education is low, substitutes for the mother's time are cheaply available, so that more educated women can enjoy the benefits of more education, such as market work or other alternative activities, without reducing fertility.

2. The small effect that exists is negative in the West.

The strong relation between education and fertility regulation also needs to be explored more fully if meaningful policies are going to be developed with respect to education. Does this relation result simply from knowledge and attitude changes or from changes resulting from status and market opportunities? Among the major questions to be answered is the extent to which mass-media campaigns and free family planning services can substitute for education in increasing contraceptive knowledge and use. These issues are fairly complex. Macro relations between education, fertility regulation, and contraceptive availability and mass-media content need to be established as well as micro relations that include data on community level family planning variables.

Testing of a complete model

All of the above factors probably operate to some extent. If education is to be considered a policy instrument to reduce fertility, the relative importance of the various aspects of education must be known. In addition, since the various characteristics of education probably operate differently on the various intervening variables, it is necessary not only to know these different effects, but also to know the relative effect of the intervening variables on completed fertility. A path analysis of the system presented in Figure 6.1 would provide such information. The amount of data necessary for such a model is, however, enormous, and therefore such a grandiose model probably will not be tested in its entirety.

Implications for Policy

The research needed to further explore the relation between education and fertility is quite substantial. Therefore, the policy conclusions that can be drawn from the existing work must be fairly tentative. First, education cannot be expected to automatically reduce fertility in all circumstances. In particular, in the poorest and least-literate societies, small amounts of education may actually lead to higher fertility initially. But there is tentative evidence that over time, education ultimately will reduce fertility. Second, increasing female education will be more likely to reduce fertility than increasing male education. Third, education is more likely to reduce fertility in urban than in rural areas.

The major policy dilemma posed by the evidence presented here is what policy should be pursued where education is unlikely to reduce fertility immediately and may in fact increase fertility in the short run. If, as hypothesized here, increases in education increase fertility by improving the health of women, increasing the perceived ability to afford children, and reducing adherence to traditional contraceptive practices such as prolonged lactation and postpartum abstinence, then it seems that even if education is not increased, fertility will rise from these factors as a result of any program to improve the well-being (health and income) of individuals and by the very process of modernization, which causes traditional behavior to be abandoned. Since the tendency for fertility to increase from these causes seems to be the inevitable product of development, the appropriate policy should be to minimize the time lag between the factors increasing fertility and the countervailing forces which tend to reduce it. Education seems to be one factor that might minimize such a lag. Once desired family size falls, it is quite evident from the literature that education enables people to better achieve these smaller sizes.

To design the best educational strategy, it is not enough to say that education should be increased despite the possibility of its immediately increasing fertility in certain circumstances. It is also necessary to know what kind of education should be increased. The direct finding of this review is that female education should receive priority. It is unclear, however, whether a broadly based program of elementary education should be recommended or a narrower program of secondary education. In the least literate countries secondary education has more immediate negative effects on fertility, but these fertility reductions will have a fairly high cost and will imply a more limited distribution of educational benefits, which is perhaps unacceptable. Policies that concentrate on mass literacy will result in initially higher individual fertility but will also raise aggregate literacy, which appears to shift the fertility increase to a fertility decrease in the long run.

Sources

•-•

INTRODUCTION AND SUMMARY

Encarnación, José, Jr. "Fertility and Labor Force Participation: Philippines 1968." *The Philippine Review of Business and Economics*, vol. 11 (December 1974).

Mason, Karen, and others. *Social and Economic Correlates of Family Fertility: A Survey of the Evidence.* Research Triangle Park, N.C.: Research Triangle Institute, 1971.

McGreevey, William P., and Nancy Birdsall. *The Policy Relevance of Recent Social Research on Fertility.* Washington, D.C.: Interdisciplinary Communications Program, Smithsonian Institute, 1974.

Simon, Julian L. *The Effects of Income on Fertility.* Chapel Hill: North Carolina Population Center, 1974.

CHAPTER 1. EDUCATION AND FERTILITY: EMPIRICAL EVIDENCE

Adelman, Irma. "An Econometric Analysis of Population Growth." *American Economic Review*, vol. 53 (June 1963), pp. 314–39.

Amani, M. *Report on the Study of the Impact of Literacy and Education on Fertility and Family Planning.* Tehran: Iran Institute for Social Studies and Research, University of Tehran, 1971.

Anker, Richard. "An Analysis of Fertility Differentials in Developing Countries." International Labor Review (ILO) Population and Employment Working Paper, no. 16. April 1975.

Anker, Richard. "The Effect of Group Level Variables on Fertility in a Rural Indian Sample." *Journal of Development Studies*, vol. 14, no. 1 (October 1977), pp. 63–76.

Becker, Gary. "A Theory of the Allocation of Time." *Economic Journal*, vol. 75 (September 1965), pp. 493–517.

Becker, Gary. "An Economic Analysis of Fertility." *Demographic and Economic Change in Developed Countries*. Princeton: National Bureau of Economic Research, 1960.

Ben-Porath, Voram. "Economic Analysis for Fertility in Israel: Point and Counterpoint." *Journal of Political Economy*, vol. 81 (March/April supplement 2, 1973), S202–233.

Bogue, Donald. *Principles and Demography*. New York: Wiley, 1969.

Caldwell, John C. *Population Growth and Family Change in Africa: The New Urban Elite in Ghana*. New York: Humanities Press, 1968.

Carelton, Robert O. "Labor Force Participation: A Stimulus to Fertility in Puerto Rico." *Demography*, vol. 2 (1965), pp. 233–39.

CELADE (United Nations Regional Center for Demographic Training and Research in Latin America) and CFSC (Community and Family Study Center). *Fertility and Family Planning in Metropolitan Latin America*. Chicago: University of Chicago, 1972.

Chernichovsky, D. "Fertility Behavior in Developing Economies: An Investment Approach." Paper presented at IUSSP Seminar on Household Models of Economic-Demographic Decision-Making, November 4–6, 1976, Mexico City. Processed.

Chernichovsky, D. "Some Socio-Economic Aspects of Fertility Behavior in Northeast Brazil: A Note." October 1976. Processed.

Chung, Bom Mo, and others. *Psychological Perspective: Family Planning in Korea*. Seoul: Hollym Corporation, 1972.

Cochrane, Susan. "The Determinants of Children Ever Born in Cross Regional Data on Thailand." Spring, 1978. Processed.

Cochrane, Susan, Bal Gopal Baidya, and Jennie Hay. "Memo on Fertility in the Parsa Pretest in Rural Nepal." World Bank, Division on Population and Human Resources, July 1977.

DaVanzo, Julie. *The Determinants of Family Formation in Chile, 1960: An Econometric Study of Female Labor Force Participation, Marriage, and Fertility Decisions*. No. R830-AID, Santa Monica, California: Rand Corporation, 1972.

Davidson, Maria. "A Comparative Study of Fertility in Mexico City and Caracas." *Social Biology*, vol. 20 (December 1973), p. 460–96.

Del Rio, A. G., W. W. Hicks, and S. R. Johnson. "Socio-Economic Determinants of Fertility in Mexico: An Analysis of Change in Structural Relationships 1950–1970." Processed.

Dow, Thomas E., Jr. "Fertility and Family Planning in Sierra Leone." *Studies in Family Planning*, vol. 2 (August 1971), pp. 153–65.

Drakatos, Constantine. "The Determinants of Birth Rate in Developing Countries: An Econometric Study of Greece." *Economic Development and Cultural Change*, vol. 17 (July 1969), pp. 596–603.

Ekanem, Ita. "A Further Note on the Relationship between Economic Development and Fertility." *Demography*, vol. 9 (August 1972), pp. 383–98.

Ekanem, Ita. "Correlates of Fertility in Eastern Nigeria." *Nigerian Journal of Economic and Social Studies* (Ibadan), vol. 16 (March 1974), pp. 115–27.

El-Badry, M. A., and Hanna Rizk. "Regional Fertility Differences among Socio-Economic Groups in the United Arab Republic." *World Population Conference, 1965*, vol. IV. New York: United Nations, 1967.

Encarnación, José, Jr. "Fertility and Labor Force Participation: Philippines 1968." *The Philippine Review of Business and Economics*, vol. 11 (December 1974).

Ewbank, Douglas. "Indicators of Fertility Levels in Tanzania: Differentials and Trends in Reported Poverty and Childlessness." Paper presented at the Annual Meeting of the Population Association of America, April 21–23, 1977, St. Louis, Missouri. Processed.

Farooq, G. M., and B. Tuncer. "Fertility and Labor Force Participation: Philippines 1968." *The Philippine Review of Business and Economics*, vol. 11 (December 1974).

Freedman, Ronald, and Bernard Berelson. "The Record of Family Planning Programs." *Studies in Family Planning*, vol. 7 (January 1977), pp. 1–40.

Friedlander, Stanley, and Morris Silver. "A Quantitative Study of the Determinants of Fertility Behavior." *Demography*, vol. 4, no. 1 (1967), pp. 30–70.

Gendell, Murray, and others. "Fertility and Economic Activity of Women in Guatemala City, 1964." *Demography*, vol. 7 (August 1970), pp. 273–86.

Goldberg, David. "Residential Location and Fertility." *Population and Development: The Search for Selected Interventions*. Edited by Ronald Ridker. Baltimore: Johns Hopkins University Press, 1976.

Goldstein, Sidney. "The Influence of Labor Force Participation and Education on Fertility in Thailand." *Population Studies*, vol. 26 (November 1972), pp. 419–36.

Gregory, Paul, John Campbell, and Benjamin Cheng. "Differences in Fertility Determinants: Developed and Developing Countries." *Journal of Development Studies*, vol. 9 (July 1973), pp. 233–41.

Hammond, John L. "Two Sources of Error in Ecological Correlations." *American Sociological Review*, vol. 38 (December 1973), pp. 764–77.

Heer, David. "Economic Development and Fertility." *Demography*, vol. 3, no. 2 (1966), pp. 423–44.

Heller, Peter S. "The Interaction of Childhood Mortality and Fertility in West Malaysia: 1947–1970." Center for Economic Development, The University of Michigan, Discussion Paper no. 57, September 1976.

Hicks, W. Whitney. "Economic Development and Fertility Change in Mexico, 1950–1970." *Demography*, vol. 11 (August 1974), pp. 407–22.

Hull, Terence, and Valerie Hull. "The Relation of Economic Class and Fertility: An Analysis of Some Indonesian Data." *Population Studies*, vol. 31 (March 1977), pp. 73–87.

Iutaka, S., E. W. Bock, and W. G. Varnes. "Factors Affecting Fertility of Natives and Migrants in Urban Brazil." *Population Studies*, vol. 25 (March 1971), pp. 55–62.

Jaffe, A. J., and K. Azumi. "The Birth Rate and Cottage Industries in Underdeveloped Countries." *Economic Development and Cultural Change*, vol. 9 (October 1960), pp. 52–63.

Janowitz, Barbara. "An Analysis of the Impact of Education on Family Size." *Demography*, vol. 13 (May 1976), pp. 189–98.

Kasarda, John D. "Economic Structure and Fertility: A Comparative Analysis." *Demography*, vol. 8 (August 1971), pp. 307–18.

Kelley, Allen. "Interaction with Economic and Demographic Household Behavior." Paper presented at National Bureau of Economic Research Conference on Population and Economic Change in Less Developed Countries, September 30–October 2, 1976. Philadelphia, Pennsylvania. Processed.

Khan, M. Ali, and Ismail Sirageldin. "Education, Income and Fertility in Pakistan." Paper presented at the Applied Research Institute, University of Karachi and Research Department of United Bank, Ltd., September 30, 1975. Processed.

Kirk, Dudley. "New Demographic Transition?" *Rapid Population*

Growth. National Academy of Sciences. Baltimore: Johns Hopkins Press, 1971.

Knodel, John, and Visid Prachuabmoh. *The Fertility of Thai Women.* Bangkok; Institute of Population Studies, Chulalongkorn University, 1973.

Knowles, James C., and Richard Anker. "Economic Determinants of Demographic Behavior in Kenya." International Labor Review (ILO) Population and Employment Working Paper no. 28, December 1975.

Kocher, James E. "Rural Development and Fertility Change in Northeast Tanzania." Paper presented at the Annual Meeting of the Population Association of America, April 21–23, 1977, St. Louis, Missouri. Processed.

Kogut, Edy Luiz. "The Economic Analysis of Fertility: A Study of Brazil." International Labor Organization (ILO) Population and Employment Working Paper no. 7, September 1974.

Lal, R. B. "Literacy and Population Growth." *Population Review,* vol. 12 (January–December 1968), pp. 55–59.

Li, W. L. "Temporal and Spatial Analysis of Fertility Decline in Taiwan." *Population Studies,* vol. 27 (March 1970), pp. 97–104.

Maurer, K., and others. *Marriage, Fertility and Labor Force Participation of Thai Women: An Econometric Study.* No. R829-AID/RF. Santa Monica, California: Rand Corporation, 1973.

McCabe, James L., and Mark R. Rosenzweig. "Female Employment Creation and Family Size." *Population and Development.* Edited by Ronald Ridker. Baltimore: Johns Hopkins University Press, 1976.

McGreevey, William P., and Nancy Birdsall. *The Policy Relevance of Recent Social Research on Fertility.* Washington, D.C.: Interdisciplinary Communications Program, Smithsonian Institute, 1974.

Merrick, Thomas. "Interregional Differences in Fertility in Brazil, 1950–1970." *Demography,* vol. 11 (August 1974), pp. 423–40.

Miro, Carmen, and Walter Mertens. "Influences Affecting Fertility in Urban and Rural Latin America." *Milbank Memorial Fund Quarterly,* vol. 46, no. 3, part 2 (July 1968), pp. 89–120.

Ohadike, Patrick. "The Possibility of Fertility Change in Modern Africa: A West African Case." *African Social Research,* vol. 8 (December 1969), pp. 602–14.

Palmore, James A., Jr. "The West Malaysian Family Survey, 1966–1967." *Studies in Family Planning,* vol. 40 (April 1969), pp. 11–20.

Repetto, Robert. "The Relationship of the Size Distribution of Income to Fertility and the Implications for Development Policy." *Population*

Policies and Economic Development. World Bank Staff Report. Edited by Timothy King. Baltimore: Johns Hopkins University Press, 1974.

Rizk, Hanna. "Trends in Fertility and Family Planning in Jordan." *Studies in Family Planning*, vol. 8 (April 1977), pp. 91–99.

Robinson, W. S. "Ecological Correlations and the Behavior of Individuals." *American Sociological Review*, vol. 15 (June 1950), pp. 351–57.

Rosenzweig, Mark R. "Rural Wages, Labor Supply and Land Reform: A Theoretical and Empirical Analysis." Discussion Paper no. 20. Research Program in Development Studies, Princeton University, December 1976.

Rule, J. R. "Fertility Differentials in India: Evidence from Rural Background." *Milbank Memorial Fund Quarterly*, vol. 41 (April 1963), pp. 183–99.

Russett, B. M. and others. *World Handbook of Social and Political Indicators*. New Haven: Yale University Press, 1964.

Safilios-Rothschild, Constantina. "Sociopsychological Factors Affecting Fertility in Urban Greece: A Preliminary Report." *Journal of Marriage and the Family*, vol. 31 (August 1969), pp. 595–606.

Schultz, T. Paul. "An Economic Model of Family Planning and Fertility." *Journal of Political Economy*, vol. 77 (March/April 1969), pp. 153–80.

Schultz, T. Paul. *Disequilibrium and Variation in Birth Rates over Space and Time: A Study of Taiwan*. Santa Monica: Rand Corporation, September 1972.

Schultz, T. Paul. "Fertility Patterns and Their Determinants in the Arab Middle East." *Economic Development and Population Growth in the Middle East*. Edited by Charles A. Cooper and Sidney Alexander. New York: Elsevier, 1972.

Siever, Daniel. "Comment on W. Whitney Hicks. Economic Development and Fertility Change in Mexico, 1950–1970." *Demography*, vol. 13 (February 1976), pp. 149–52.

Simmons, Alan B., and Johanna de Jong. "Education and Contraception in Rural Latin America." Processed.

Srinivasan, K. "A Prospective Study of the Fertility Behavior of a Group of Married Women in Rural India—Design and Findings of the First Round of Enquiry." *Population Review*, vol. 11 (July–December 1967), pp. 46–60.

Stycos, J. Mayone. *Human Fertility in Latin America*. Ithaca: Cornell University Press, 1968.

Stycos, J., and Robert Weller. "Female Working Roles and Fertility." *Demography*, vol. 4, no. 1 (1967), pp. 210–17.

Timur, Serim. "Demographic Correlates of Woman's Education: Fertility Age at Marriage, and the Family." Paper presented at 18th General Conference of the International Union for the Scientific Study of Population, August 8–13, 1977, Mexico City.

Traina, Frank J., and Herman D. Bontrager. "Statistical Determinants of Fertility Decline in Costa Rica." Paper presented at the Annual Meeting of the Population Association of America, April 21–23, 1977, St. Louis, Missouri. Processed.

Willis, Robert J. "A New Approach to the Economic Theory of Fertility Behavior." *Journal of Political Economy*, vol. 81 (March/April 1973), pp. 514–69.

World Bank. "Population Policies and Economic Development." World Bank Staff Report. Baltimore: Johns Hopkins University Press, 1974.

World Fertility Survey. "Nepal Fertility Survey, 1976, First Report." Kathmandu, 1977.

World Fertility Survey. "The Survey of Fertility in Thailand." Country Report, vol. 1. Institute of Population Studies. Bangkok, 1977.

Yaukey, David. "Some Immediate Determinants of Fertility Differences in Lebanon." *Marriage and Family Living*, vol. 25 (February 1963), pp. 27–33.

Zarate, Celvan. "Fertility in Urban Areas of Mexico: Implications for the Theory of Demographic Transition." *Demography*, vol. 4, no. 1 (1977), pp. 363–73.

CHAPTER 2. THE THEORETICAL DETERMINANTS OF FERTILITY

Arnold, Fred, and others. *The Value of Children: A Cross-National Survey. Vol. 1, Introduction and Comparative Analysis.* Honolulu: The East–West Center, 1975.

Baird, Dugald. "Variation in Fertility Associated with Changes in Health Status." *Public Health and Population Change.* Pittsburgh: University of Pittsburgh Press, 1965.

Bean, Frank, Susan Cochrane, Howard Savage, and Charles Wood. "The Effect of Income on the Demand for and/or Supply of Children." *Research in Population Economics.* Edited by Julian Simon. Vol. 1. Greenwich, Conn.: JAI Press, 1976.

Bindary, A., and others. "Urban–Rural Differences in the Relationship between Women's Employment and Fertility." *Journal of Biosocial Science*, vol. 5 (1973), pp. 159–67

Bulatao, Rodolfo. *The Value of Children: A Cross-National Survey. Vol. 2, The Philippines.* Honolulu: The East–West Center, 1975.

Butz, William P., and Jean-Pierre Habicht. "The Effects of Nutrition and Health on Fertility: Hypotheses, Evidence and Intervention." *Population and Development: The Search for Selective Interventions.* Edited by Ronald Ridker. Baltimore: Johns Hopkins University Press, 1976.

Cain, Glen, and Adriana Weinenger. "Economic Determinants of Fertility: Results from Cross-Sectional Aggregate Data." *Demography,* vol. 10 (May 1973), pp. 205–21.

Carelton, Robert O. "Labor Force Participation: A Stimulus to Fertility in Puerto Rico." *Demography,* no. 2 (1965), pp. 233–39.

Cho, Lee-Jay, and Robert D. Rutherford. "Comparative Analysis of Recent Fertility Trends in East Asia." *Proceedings at the International Union for the Scientific Study of Population (I.U.S.S.P.),* vol. 2, pp. 163–81. Liege, 1973.

Cochrane, Susan, and James Cochrane. "Child, Mortality and the Desired Number of Children and Births." *Australian Economic Papers* (June 1974).

DaVanzo, Julie. *The Determinants of Family Formation in Chile, 1960: The Econometric Study of Female Labor Force Participation, Marriage and Fertility Decisions.* No. R830-AID. Santa Monica, California: Rand Corporation, 1972.

Davidson, Maria. "A Comparative Study of Fertility in Mexico City and Caracas." *Social Biology,* vol. 20 (December 1973), pp. 460–96.

Davis, Kingsley, and Judith Blake. "Social Structure and Fertility: An Analytical Framework." *Economic Development and Cultural Change,* vol. 4 (1956), pp. 211–35.

Duza, M. Badrud, and C. Stephen Baldwin. "Nuptiality as an Area for Policy Intervention: A Comparative Perspective." Adapted from *Nuptiality and Population Policy: An Investigation in Sri Lanka, Malaysia and Bangladesh.* New York Population Council, 1974.

Easterlin, Richard A. "An Economic Framework for Fertility Analysis." *Studies in Family Planning,* vol. 6 (March 3, 1975), pp. 54–63.

Easterlin, Richard A. "Toward a Socio-Economic Theory of Fertility: Survey of Recent Research on Economic Factors in American Fertility." *Fertility and Family Planning: A World View.* Ann Arbor: University of Michigan Press, 1969.

Easterlin, Richard A., Robert A. Pollack, and Michael L. Wachter. "Toward A More General Economic Model of Fertility Determination: Endogenous Preferences and Natural Fertility." Presented at the National Bureau of Economic Research Conference on Economic and Demographic Change in Less Developed Countries, September 30–October 2, 1976, Philadelphia. Processed.

Encarnación, José. "Fertility and Labor Force Participation: Philippines 1968." *The Philippine Review of Business and Economics,* vol. 11 (December 1974).

Freedman, R., and L. Coombs. *Cross-Cultural Comparisons: Data on Two Factors in Fertility Behavior.* New York: The Population Council, 1974.

Freedman, R. and others. "Hong Kong's Fertility Decline, 1961–68." *Population Index,* vol. 36 (January–March, 1970).

Galbraith, John Kenneth. "The Economics of the American Housewife." *The Atlantic Monthly,* vol. 232 (1973), pp. 78–83.

Goldstein, Sidney. "The Influence of Labor Force Participation and Education on Fertility in Thailand." *Population Studies,* vol. 26 (November 1972), pp. 419–36.

Haas, Paula. "Wanted and Unwanted Pregnancies: A Fertility Decision-Making Model." *Journal of Social Forces,* vol. 30 (1974), pp. 125–65.

Harmon, Alvin. *Fertility and Economic Behavior of Families in the Philippines.* Santa Monica, California: Rand Corporation, September 1970.

Heckman, James I., and Robert J. Willis. "Estimation of a Stochastic Model of Reproduction: An Econometric Approach." *Household Production and Consumption.* Edited by Nestor Terleckyj. New York: National Bureau of Economic Research, 1976.

Hill, Rueben and others. *The Family and Population Control.* Chapel Hill: University of North Carolina Press, 1959.

Holsinger, Donald B., and John D. Kasarda. "Education and Human Fertility: Sociological Perspectives." *Population and Development: The Search for Selective Intervention.* Baltimore: Johns Hopkins University Press, 1976.

Kim, Mo-Im. "Age at Marriage, Family Planning Practices and Other Variables as Correlates of Fertility in Korea." *Demography,* vol. 1 (November 1977), pp. 413–28.

Mason, Karen and others. *Social and Economic Correlates of Family Fertility: A Survey of the Evidence.* Research Triangle Park, N.C.: Research Triangle Institute, 1971.

Maurer, K. and others. *Marriage, Fertility and Labor Force Participation of Thai Women: An Econometric Study.* No. R829-AID/RF. Santa Monica, California: Rand Corporation, 1973.

Mazur, D. P. "Relation of Marriage and Education to Fertility in the USSR." *Population Studies,* vol. 27, no. 1 (March 1973), pp. 105–15.

McCabe, James L., and Mark Rosenzweig. "Female Employment Creation and Family Size." *Population and Development.* Edited by Ronald Ridker. Baltimore: Johns Hopkins University Press, 1976.

McGreevey, W. P., and Nancy Birdsall. *The Policy Relevance of Recent Social Research on Fertility*. Washington, D.C.: Interdisciplinary Communications Program, Smithsonian Institute, 1974.

Michael, Robert T. "Education and the Derived Demand for Children." *Journal of Political Economy*, vol. 8 (March/April 1973), Supplement: S128–S164.

Michael, Robert T., and R. J. Willis. "Contraception and Fertility: Household Production under Uncertainty." *Household Production and Consumption*. Edited by Nestor Terleckyj. New York: National Bureau of Economic Research, 1976.

Michel, A. "Interaction and Family Planning in the French Urban Family." *Demography*, vol. 4, no. 2 (1967), pp. 615–25.

Miro, Carmen, and Walter Mertens. "Influences Affecting Fertility in Urban and Rural Latin America." *Milbank Memorial Fund Quarterly*, vol. 46, no. 3, part 2 (July 1968), pp. 89–120.

Mitchell, Robert E. "Husband-Wife Relations and Family Planning Practice in Urban Hong Kong." *Journal of Marriage and Family*, vol. 34 (February 1972), pp. 139–46.

Mueller, Eva. "Economic Motivations for Family Limitation." *Demography*, vol. 26, no. 3 (November 1972), pp. 383–403.

Namboodiri, N. Krishnan. "Some Observations on the Economic Framework for Fertility Analysis." *Population Studies*, vol. 26 (July 1972·), pp. 175–206.

Nerlove, Marc. "Household and Economy toward A New Theory of Population and Economic Growth." *Journal of Political Economy*, vol. 82 (March/April 1974), Supplement S200–S218.

Nerlove, Marc, and Paul T. Schultz. "Love and Life between the Censuses: Model of Family Decision-Making in Puerto Rico, 1950–1960." No. RM-6322-AID. Santa Monica, California: Rand Corporation, 1970. Processed.

Palmore, James A., and M. Ariffin. "Marriage Patterns and Cumulative Fertility in West Malaysia: 1966–1967." *Demography*, vol. 6 (November 1969), pp. 383–401.

Ramakumar, S. R., and S. V. S. Gopal. "Husband-Wife Communications and Fertility in a Suburban Community Exposed to Family Planning." *Journal of Family Welfare*, vol. 18 (March 1972), pp. 30–36.

Repetto, Robert. "Inequality and the Birth Rate in Puerto Rico: Evidence from Household Census Data." Research Paper no. 14. Harvard University Center for Population Studies. June 1976.

Rosen, Bernard C., and Alan B. Simmons. "Industrialization, Family and Fertility: A Structural–Psychological Analysis of the Brazilian Case." *Demography*, vol. 8 (February 1971), pp. 49–69.

Rosenzweig, Mark R., and Robert Evenson. "Fertility, Schooling and the Economic Contribution of Children in Rural India: An Econometric Analysis."*Econometrica*, vol. 45 (July 1977), pp. 1065–79.

Samuelson, Paul A. "Social Indifference Curves." *Quarterly Journal of Economics*, vol. 70 (February 1956), pp. 1–22.

Schultz, T. Paul. "Fertility Patterns and Their Determinants in the Arab Middle East." *Economic Development and Population Growth in the Middle East.* Edited by Charles Cooper and Sidney Alexander. New York: Elsevier, 1972.

Shields, Nwanganga. "Female Labor Force Participation and Fertility: Review of Empirical Evidence." Draft for Population and Human Resources Division, Development Economics Department. World Bank, February 1977.

Simon, Julian L. *The Effects of Income on Fertility.* Chapel Hill: North Carolina Population Center, 1974.

Snyder, Donald W. "The Economic Determinants of Family Size in West Africa." *Demography*, vol. 11 (November 1974), pp. 613–28.

Turchi, Boone. "Micro-Economic Theories of Fertility." *Social Forces*, vol. 54 (September 1975), pp. 107–25.

United Nations. *The Determinants and Consequences of Population Trends.* New York: United Nations, 1973.

Weller, Robert. "The Employment of Wives, Role Incompatibility and Fertility: A Study among the Lower and Middle Class Residents of San Juan, Puerto Rico." *Milbank Memorial Fund Quarterly*, vol. 46 (October 1968), pp. 507–26.

Williams, Anne D. "Review and Evaluation of the Literature." *Population, Public Policy and Economic Development.* Edited by Michael C. Keeby. New York: Praeger, 1976.

Yaukey, David, and Timm Thorsen. "Differential Female Days at First Marriage in Six Latin American Cities." *Journal of Marriage and the Family* (May 1972), pp. 375–79.

CHAPTER 3.   EDUCATION AND THE BIOLOGICAL SUPPLY OF CHILDREN: EMPIRICAL EVIDENCE

Adegbola, H. J. Page, and R. Lesthaeghe. "Breastfeeding and Post Partum Abstinence in Metropolitan Lagos." Paper presented at the Annual Meeting of the Population Association of America, April 21–23, 1977, St. Louis, Missouri. Processed.

Amani, M. *Report on the Study of the Impact of Library and Education on Fertility and Family Planning.* Tehran: Institute for Social Studies and Research, University of Tehran, 1971.

Baird, Dugald. "Variation in Fertility Associated with Changes in Health Status." *Public Health and Population Change.* Pittsburgh: University of Pittsburgh Press, 1965.

Butz, William P., and Julie DaVanzo. "Contracepting, Breastfeeding and Birthspacing in Malaysia: A Model of Decision-Making Subject to Economic and Biological Constraints." A preliminary paper. Rand Corporation, April 1978.

Butz, William P., and Jean-Pierre Habicht. "The Effects of Nutrition and Health on Fertility: Hypotheses, Evidence and Intervention." *Population and Development: The Search For Selective Interventions.* Edited by Ronald Ridker. Baltimore: Johns Hopkins University Press, 1976.

Caldwell, John C. *Population of Growth and Family Change in Africa: The New Urban Elite in Ghana.* New York: Humanities Press, 1968.

CELADE (United Nations Regional Center for Demographic Training and Research in Latin America) and CFSC (Community and Family Study Center). *Fertility and Family Planning in Metropolitan Latin America.* Chicago: University of Chicago, 1972.

Chander, R., and V. T. Palan. *Malaysian Fertility and Family Survey 1974: First Country Report.* Kuala Lumpur: Department of Statistics, 1977.

Chojnacka, Helena. "Nuptiality Patterns in an Agrarian Society." *Population Studies,* vol. 30 (July 1976), pp. 203–27.

Chung, Bom Mo, and others. *Psychological Perspectives: Family Planning in Korea.* Seoul: Hollym Corporation, 1972.

Cochrane, Susan, Bal Gopal Baidya, and Jennie Hay. "Memo on Fertility in the Parsa Pretest in Rural Nepal." World Bank, Division on Population and Human Resources, July 1977.

DaVanzo, Julie. *The Determinants of Family Formation in Chile, 1960: An Econometric Study of Female Labor Force Participation, Marriage, and Fertility Decisions.* No. R830-AID. Santa Monica, California: Rand Corporation, 1972.

Dixon, Ruth. "Explaining Cross Cultural Variations in Age of Marriage and Proportion Never Marrying." *Population Studies,* vol. 25 (July 1971), pp. 215–33.

Harmon, Alvin. *Fertility and Economic Behavior of Families in the Philippines.* Santa Monica, California: Rand Corporation, September 1970.

Hawley, Amos, and Visid Prachuabmoh. "Family Growth and Family Planning in a Rural District of Thailand." *Family Planning and Population Programs.* Edited by Bernard Berelson and others. Chicago: University of Chicago Press, 1966.

Heller, Peter S. "The Interaction of Childhood Mortality and Fertility in West Malaysia: 1947–1970." Discussion Paper no. 57. Center for Economic Development, University of Michigan. September 1976.

Hull, Terence, and Valerie Hull. "The Relation of Economic Class and Fertility: An Analysis of Some Indonesian Data." *Population Studies*, vol. 31 (March 1977), pp. 73–87.

Jain, Anrudh K. "Socio-Economic Correlates of Fecundability in a Sample of Taiwanese Women." *Demography*, vol. 6 (February 1969), pp. 75–90.

Jain, Anrudh K., T. C. Hsu, R. Freedman, and M. C. Chang. "Demographic Aspects of Lactation and Postpartum Amenorrhea." *Demography*, vol. 7 (May 1970), pp. 255–71.

Kelley, Allen. "Interaction of Economic and Demographic Household Behavior." Paper presented at National Bureau of Economic Research Conference on Population and Economic Change in Less Developed Countries, September 30–October 2, 1976. Philadelphia, Pennsylvania. Processed.

Khalifa, Atef M. "The Influence of Wife's Education on Fertility in Rural Egypt." *Journal of Biosocial Science*, vol. 8 (January 1976), pp. 53–60.

Khan, M. Ali, and Ismail Sirageldin. "Education, Income and Fertility in Pakistan." Paper presented at the Applied Research Institute, University of Karachi and the Research Department of United Bank Ltd., September 30, 1975. Processed.

Knowles, James C., and Richard Anker. "Economic Determinants of Demographic Behavior in Kenya." International Labor Review (ILO) Population and Employment Working Paper no. 28, December 1975.

Kogut, Edy Luiz. "The Economic Analysis of Fertility: A Study of Brazil." International Labor Organization (ILO) Population and Employment Working paper no. 7, September 1974.

Lapierre-Adamcyk, E., and T. Burch. "Trends and Differentials in Age of Marriage in Korea." *Studies in Family Planning*, vol. 5 (August 1972), pp. 255–60.

Maurer, K. and others. *Marriage, Fertility and Labor Force Participation of Thai Women: An Econometric Study.* No. R829-AID/RF. Santa Monica, California: Rand Corporation, 1973.

Mott, Frank. "Socio-Economic Determinants of Fertility in a Nigerian Village." 1976. Processed.

Nayar, P. K. B. "The Influence of Education on Fertility." *Journal of Family Welfare* (Bombay), vol. 20 (March 1974), pp. 28–36.

Olusanya, P. O. "Status Differentials in the Fertility Attitudes of Married Women in Two Communities in Western Nigeria." *Economic Development and Cultural Change*, vol. 19, no. 4 (July 1971), pp. 641–51.

Palmore, James A., and M. Ariffin. "Marriage Patterns and Cumulative Fertility in West Malaysia: 1966–1967." *Demography*, vol. 6 (November 1969), pp. 383–401.

Paydurfar, Ali A. "Sociocultural Correlates of Fertility among Tribal, Rural and Urban Populations in Iran." *Social Biology*, vol. 22 (Summer 1975), pp. 151–66.

Shin, Eui Hang. "Economic and Social Correlates of Infant Mortality: A Cross Sectional and Longitudinal Analysis of 63 Selected Countries." *Social Biology*, vol. 22, no. 4 (Winter 1975), pp. 315–25.

Singh, K. P. "Child Mortality, Social Status and Fertility in India." *Social Biology*, vol. 21, no. 4 (Winter 1974), pp. 385–88.

Sloan, Frank. *Survival of Progeny in Developing Countries: An Analysis of Evidence from Costa Rica, Mexico, East Pakistan and Puerto Rico*. Santa Monica, California: Rand Corporation, 1971.

Smith, Peter C. "Tradition and Transition in South and Southeast and East Asian Nuptiality." Paper presented at the 1977 Annual Meeting of the Population Association of America, April 21–23, 1977, St. Louis, Missouri. Processed.

Speare, Alden, Jr. and others. "Urbanization, Non-Familial Work, Education and Fertility in Taiwan." *Population Studies*, vol. 27 (July 1973), pp. 323–34.

Stockwell, E. G., and B. W. Hutchinson. "A Note on Mortality Correlate of Economic Development." *Population Review*, vol. 19 (January–December 1975), pp. 46–50.

Stycos, J. Mayone. *Human Fertility in Latin America*. Ithaca: Cornell University Press, 1968.

Stycos, J., and Robert Weller. "Female Working Roles and Fertility." *Demography*, vol. 4, no. 1 (1967), pp. 210–17.

World Fertility Survey. "Nepal Fertility Survey, 1976, First Report." Kathmandu, 1977.

Yaukey, David. "Some Immediate Determinants of Fertility Differences in Lebanon." *Marriage and Family Living*, vol. 25 (February 1963), pp. 27–33.

Yaukey, David and Timm Thorsen. "Differential Female Age at First Marriage in Six Latin American Cities." *Journal of Marriage and the Family* (May 1972), pp. 375–79.

CHAPTER 4. EDUCATION AND THE DEMAND FOR CHILDREN: EMPIRICAL
EVIDENCE

Arnold, Fred, and others. *The Value of Children: A Cross-National Study.
Vol. 1, Introduction and Comparative Analysis.* Honolulu: The East–
West Center, 1975.

Becker, Gary. "An Economic Analysis of Fertility." *Demographic and
Economic Change in Developed Countries.* Princeton: National Bureau
of Economic Research, 1960.

Bulatao, Rodolfo. *The Value of Children: A Cross-National Survey. Vol.
2, The Philippines.* Honolulu: The East–West Center, 1975.

CELADE (United Nations Center for Demographic Training and Research
in Latin America) and CFSC (Community and Family Study Center).
Fertility and Family Planning in Metropolitan Latin America. Chicago:
University of Chicago, 1972.

Chang, Cheng-Tung. "Desired Fertility, Income and the Valuation of
Children." International Labor Organization (ILO), Population and
Employment Working Paper no. 36, March 1976.

Chung, Bom Mo, and others. *Psychological Perspectives: Family Planning
in Korea.* Seoul: Hollym Corporation, 1972.

Coombs, Lolagene. *Are Cross-Cultural Preference Comparisons Possible?
A Measurement-Theoretic Approach.* IUSSP Paper no. 5. Liege, Belgium: International Union for the Scientific Study of Population, 1975.

Dow, Thomas E., Jr. "Fertility and Family Planning in Sierra Leone."
Studies in Family Planning, vol. 2 (August 1971), pp. 153–65.

Freedman, R., and L. Coombs. *Cross-Cultural Comparisons: Data on
Two Factors in Fertility Behavior.* New York: The Population Council,
1974.

Freedman, R., L. Coombs, M. Chang, and T. H. Sun. "Trends in Fertility, Family Size Preferences and Practices of Family Planning:
Taiwan, 1965–73." *Studies in Family Planning,* vol. 5 (September
1974), pp. 270–88.

Freedman, R., D. Goldberg, and Sharp. "Ideals about Family Size in the
Detroit Metropolitan Area, 1954." *Milbank Memorial Fund Quarterly,*
vol. 33 (1955), pp. 187–95.

Freedman, R., J. Y. Peng, Y. Takeshito, and T. H. Sun. "Fertility Trends
in Taiwan: Transition and Change." *Population Studies,* vol. 16
(March 1963), pp. 219–36.

Khalifa, Atef M. "A Proposed Explanation of the Fertility Gap Differentials by Socio-Economic Status and Modernity: The Case of Egypt."
Population Studies, vol. 27 (November 1973), pp. 431–42.

Knodel, John, and Pichit Pitakepsombati. "Thailand: Fertility and Family Planning among Rural and Urban Women." *Studies in Family Planning*, vol. 4 (September 1973), pp. 229–55.

Leibenstein, Harvey. *Economic Backwardness and Economic Growth.* New York: John Wiley and Sons, 1957.

Maurer, K., and others. *Marriage, Fertility and Labor Force Participation of Thai Women: An Economic Study.* No. R829-AID/RF. Santa Monica, California: Rand Corporation, 1973.

Mueller, Eva. "Economic Motivations for Family Limitation." *Demography*, vol. 26, no. 3 (November 1972), pp. 383–403.

Mueller, Eva, and Richard Cohn. "The Relation of Income to Fertility Decisions in Taiwan." *Economic Development and Cultural Change*, vol. 25 (January 1977), pp. 325–47.

Ohadike, Patrick. "The Possibility of Fertility Change in Modern Africa: A West African Case." *African Social Research*, vol. 8 (December 1969), pp. 602–14.

Olusanya, P. O. "Status Differentials in the Fertility Attitudes of Married Women in Two Communities in Western Nigeria." *Economic Development and Cultural Change*, vol. 19, no. 4 (July 1971), pp. 641–51.

Palmore, James, and M. Ariffin. "Marriage Patterns and Cumulative Fertility in West Malaysia: 1966–1967." *Demography* (November 1969), pp. 383–401.

Pareek, Udai, and V. Kothandapani. "Modernization and Attitude toward Family Size and Family Planning: Analysis of Some Data from India." *Social Biology*, vol. 16 (March 1969), pp. 44–48.

Paydarfar, Ali A. "Sociocultural Correlates of Fertility among Tribal, Rural, and Urban Populations in Iran." *Social Biology*, vol. 22 (Summer 1975), pp. 151–66.

Pool, D. I. "Social Change and Interest in Family Planning in Ghana: An Exploratory Analysis." *Canadian Journal of African Studies*, vol. 4 (Spring 1970), pp. 209–27.

Rizk, Hanna. "Trends in Fertility and Family Planning in Jordan." *Studies in Family Planning*, vol. 8 (April 1977), pp. 91–99.

Rosenzweig, Mark R. "Rural Wages, Labor Supply and Land Reform: A Theoretical and Empirical Analysis." Discussion Paper no. 20. Research Program in Development Studies, Princeton University, December 1976.

Speare, Alden Jr., and others. "Urbanization, Non-Familial Work, Education and Fertility in Taiwan." *Population Studies*, vol. 27 (July 1973), pp. 323–34.

Ware, Helen. "Ideal Family Size." World Fertility Survey Occasional Paper no. 13. October 1974.

Ware, Helen. "The Limits of Acceptable Family Size in Western Nigeria." *Journal of Biosocial Services*, vol. 7 (1975), pp. 273–96.

Weekes–Vaglioni, Winifred. *Family Life and Structure in Southern Cameroon*. Paris: Development Centre of Office of Economic Cooperation and Development, 1976.

Willis, Robert J. "A New Approach to the Economic Theory of Fertility Behavior." *Journal of Political Economy*, vol. 81 (no. 2, part II—March/April 1973), pp. 514–564.

World Fertility Survey. "Nepal Fertility Survey, 1976. First Report." Kathmandu, 1977.

World Fertility Survey. "The Survey of Fertility in Thailand: Country Report," vol. 1. Institute of Population Studies, Bangkok, 1977.

Yaukey, David. "Some Immediate Determinants of Fertility Differences in Lebanon." *Marriage and Family Living*, vol. 25 (February 1963), pp. 27–33.

CHAPTER 5: EDUCATION AND FERTILITY REGULATION: EMPIRICAL EVIDENCE

Arnold, Fred and others. *The Value of Children: A Cross-National Study, Vol. 1, Introduction and Comparative Analysis*. Honolulu: The East–West Center, 1975.

Brody, Eugene B., Frank Ottey, and Janet La Granade. "Fertility-Related Behavior in Jamaica." *Cultural Factors and Population in Developing Countries*. Occasional Monograph no. 6. International Communications Program. Washington, D.C.: Smithsonian Institute, 1977.

Caldwell, John C. (ed.). *Population Growth and Socio-Economic Change in West Africa*. New York: Columbia University Press, 1975.

Caldwell, John C., and A. Igun. "Anti-Natal Knowledge and Practice in Nigeria." *Population Growth and Economic Development in Africa*. Edited by S. H. Ominde and C. N. Ejigu. London: Heineman, 1972, pp. 67–76.

CELADE (United Nations Regional Center for Demographic Training and Research in Latin America) and CFSC (Community and Fertility Study Center). *Fertility and Family Planning in Metropolitan Latin America*. Chicago: University of Chicago, 1972.

Chung, Bom Mo, and others. *Psychological Perspectives: Family Planning in Korea*. Seoul: Hollym Corporation, 1972.

Dow, Thomas E., Jr. "Fertility and Family Planning in Sierra Leone." *Studies in Family Planning*. Vol. 2 (August 1971), pp. 153–65.

Freedman, R., and L. Coombs. *Cross-Cultural Comparisons: Data on Two Factors in Fertility Behavior*. New York: The Population Council, 1974.

Freedman, R., J. Y. Peng, Y. Takeshito, and T. H. Sun. "Fertility Trends in Taiwan: Transition and Change." *Population Studies*, vol. 16 (March 1963), pp. 219–36.

Goldberg, David, and Greer Litton. "Family Planning: Observations and an Interpretive Scheme." *Turkish Demography: Proceedings of a Conference*. Edited by Frederic S. Shorter and Bozkurt Guvenc Hacettepe University, 1967, pp. 214–48.

Hill, Reuben, and others. *The Family and Population Control*. Chapel Hill: University of North Carolina Press, 1959.

Khalifa, Atef M. "A Proposed Explanation of the Fertility Gap Differentials by Socio-Economic Status and Modernity: The Case of Egypt." *Population Studies*, vol. 27 (November 1973), pp. 431–42.

Khalifa, Atef M. "The Influence of Wife's Education on Fertility in Rural Egypt." *Journal of Biosocial Science*, vol. 8 (January 1976), pp. 53–60.

Knodel, John, and Pichit Pitakepsombati. "Thailand: Fertility and Family Planning among Rural and Urban Women." *Studies in Family Planning*, vol. 4 (September 1973), pp. 229–55.

Michel, A. "Interaction and Family Planning in the French Urban Family." *Demography*, vol. 4, no. 2 (1967), pp. 615–25.

Mitchell, Robert E. "Husband-Wife Relations and Family Planning Practice in Urban Hong Kong." *Journal of Marriage and Family*, vol. 34 (February 1972), pp. 139–46.

Morgan, Robert W. "Fertility Levels and Fertility Change." *Population Growth and Socioeconomic Change in West Africa*. Edited by John C. Caldwell and others. New York: Columbia University Press, 1975, pp. 187–238.

Morrison, William. "Family Planning Attitudes of Industrial Workers of Ambornath, A City in Western India." *Population Studies*, vol. 14 (March 1961), pp. 235–48.

Mueller, Eva, and Richard Cohn. "The Relation of Income to Fertility Decisions in Taiwan." *Economic Development and Cultural Change*, vol. 25 (January 1977), pp. 325–47.

Mukherjee, B. N. "The Role of Husband-Wife Communications in Family Planning." *Journal of Marriage and the Family*, vol. 37 (August 1975), pp. 655–67.

Nepal Family Planning. "Fertility, Family Planning and Desire for Children." Four District Baseline Survey Report no. 1. His Majesty's Government Ministry of Health. Kathmandu, Nepal.

Olusanya, P. O. "Status Differentials in the Fertility Attitudes of Married Women in Two Communities in Western Nigeria." *Economic Development and Cultural Change*, vol. 19, no. 4 (July 1971), pp. 641–51.

Oppong, Christine. "Conjugal Power and Resources: An Urban African Example." *Journal of Marriage and the Family* (November 1970), pp. 676–80.

Palmore, James A., Jr. "The West Malaysian Family Survey, 1966–1967." *Studies in Family Planning*, vol. 40 (April 1969), pp. 11–20.

Pareek, Udai, and V. Kothandapani. "Modernization and Attitude toward Family Size and Family Planning: Analysis of Some Data from India." *Social Biology*, vol. 16 (March 1969), pp. 44–48.

Pool, D. I. "Social Change and Interest in Family Planning in Ghana: An Exploratory Analysis." *Canadian Journal of African Studies*, vol. 4 (Spring 1970), pp. 209–27.

Ramakumar, S. R., and S. V. S. Gopal. "Husband-Wife Communications and Fertility in a Suburban Community Exposed to Family Planning." *Journal of Family Welfare*, vol. 18 (March 1972), pp. 30–36.

Roberts, J. B., and others. "Family Planning Survey in Dacca, East Pakistan." *Demography*, vol. 2 (1965), pp. 74–96.

Sear, Alan M. "Predictors of Contraceptive Practice for Low Income Women in Cali, Colombia." *Journal of Biosocial Science*, vol. 7 (1975), pp. 171–88.

Simmons, Alan B., and Mauricio Culagovski. "If They Know, Why Don't They Use? Selected Factors Influencing Contraceptive Adoption in Rural Latin America." April, 1975. Processed.

Simmons, Alan B., and Johanna de Jong. "Education and Contraception in Rural Latin America." Processed.

Speare, Alden Jr., and others. "Urbanization, Non-Familial Work, Education and Fertility in Taiwan." *Population Studies*, vol. 27 (July 1973), pp. 323–34.

Williamson, John B. "Subjective Efficiency and Ideal Family Size as Predictors of Favorability toward Birth Control." *Demography*, vol. 7 (August 1970), pp. 329–39.

World Fertility Survey. "Nepal Fertility Survey, 1976. First Report." Kathmandu, 1977.

Yaukey, David. "Some Immediate Determinants of Fertility Differences in Lebanon." *Marriage and Family Living*, vol. 25 (February 1963), pp. 27–33.

CHAPTER 6. EDUCATION AND FERTILITY: SUMMARY AND IMPLICATIONS FOR RESEARCH AND POLICY

Leibenstein, Harvey. "Beyond Economic Man: Economics, Politics, and the Population Problem." *Population and Development Review*, vol. 3 (September 1977), pp. 183–99.

Author Index

Farooq, G. M., 16
Freedman, Ronald, 17, 19, 20, 58n, 77, 102n, 103, 104, 106n, 107, 112, 113, 118, 127, 129, 133, 137
Friedlander, Stanley, 16, 17, 19, 20, 21, 22

Galbraith, John Kenneth, 58
Gendell, Murray, 37
Goldberg, David, 31n, 102n, 133n
Goldstein, Sidney, 34, 37, 67, 78
Gopal, S. V. S., 67, 123, 124
Gregory, Paul, 16, 18, 19, 20

Haas, Paula, 56, 61
Habicht, Jean-Pierre, 91n
Hammond, John L., 32n
Harmon, Alvin, 67, 86, 90
Hawley, Amos, 84, 87
Heckman, James I., 57
Heer, David, 15, 17, 18, 19, 20
Heller, Peter S., 16, 94, 95, 96
Hicks, W. Whitney, 16, 23, 24, 26
Hill, Reuben, 67, 123
Holsinger, Donald B., 55, 61
Hull, Terence, 37, 92, 94, 97
Hull, Valerie, 92, 94, 97
Hutchinson, B. W., 93, 94, 95

Igun, A., 120, 130
Iutaka, S., 44

Jaffe, A. J., 33n, 42n
Jain, Anrudh K., 91, 92
Janowitz, Barbara, 16, 17, 18, 19, 20, 21

Kasarda, John D., 15, 17, 18, 55, 61
Kelley, Allen, 46, 94
Khalifa, Atef M., 94, 97, 103, 104, 118, 120, 124, 126
Khan, M. Ali, 44
Khan, Z., 94, 97
Kim, Mo-Im, 66
Kirk, Dudley, 15, 16, 17, 18, 21, 41
Knodel, John, 36, 103, 104, 117, 118, 120, 125, 126
Knowles, James C., 46, 86, 90, 95

Kocher, James E., 46
Kogut, Edy Suiz, 44, 86, 90
Kothandapani, V., 103, 105, 119

Lal, R. B., 16
Lapierre-Adamcyk, E., 84, 88, 89
Leibenstein, Harvey, 107, 141
Li, W. L., 17, 24
Litton, Greer, 133n

Mason, Karen, 3, 4, 65, 66, 67, 68
Maurer, K., 66, 81, 82, 102n
Mazur, D. P., 66
McCabe, James L., 16, 18, 19, 20, 21, 44
McGreevey, William P., 3, 4, 65, 66, 67
Merrick, Thomas, 16, 22, 24
Mertens, Walter, 32, 42n, 66
Michael, Robert T., 57
Michel, A., 67, 123
Miro, Carmen, 32, 42n, 66
Mitchell, Robert E., 65, 67, 123
Morgan, Robert W., 118
Morrison, William, 117, 119, 120
Mott, Frank, 84, 87
Mueller, Eva, 58n, 67, 69, 109, 110, 135
Mukherjee, B. N., 123, 124

Namboodiri, N. Krishnan, 56, 61
Nayar, P. K. B., 84, 88
Nerlove, Marc, 58, 66

Ohadike, Patrick, 38, 105, 130, 131
Olusanya, P. O., 85, 87, 95, 97, 104, 105, 109, 124, 130
Oppong, Christine, 124

Palan, V. T., 84, 92
Palmore, James A., Jr., 37, 66, 85, 112, 113, 117, 119, 120, 125, 126
Pareek, Udai, 103, 105, 119
Paydarfar, Ali A., 86, 89, 113, 114
Pitakepsombati, Pichit, 103, 104, 117, 118, 120, 125, 126
Pool, D. I., 112, 113, 119, 121, 124
Prachuabmoh, Visid, 36, 84, 87